SIGNIFICANT AMERICAN SCIENTISTS

Childrens Press
Chicago, Illinois

T780

CREDITS

EXECUTIVE EDITOR

ALVIN W. QUINN, ED.D.
Science Department
Northeastern Illinois University
Chicago, Illinois

CONSULTANTS

MORRIS R. BUSKE, M.A.
Triton College, River Grove, Illinois

GILBERT MIEKINA, M.A.T.
Southwestern Central High School, Jamestown, New York

JACK KENT MANDEL, M.B.A.
John Wilson Jr. High School, Brooklyn, New York

IDA S. MELTZER, B.S.
Marine Park Jr. High School, Brooklyn, New York

RESEARCH AND PRODUCTION

THOMAS McLAUGHLIN

ROBERT GOLDIN

JOSEPH POSTILION

NICK CURCIO

RONALD FALK

Library of Congress Cataloging in Publication Data
Main entry under title:

Significant American scientists.

Includes index.
SUMMARY: Brief biographies of 166 American scientists
arranged alphabetically within broad chronological
periods of American history.
1. Scientists—United States—Biography—Juvenile
literature. [1. Scientists] I. Title: Scientists.
Q141.S485   509′.2′2 [B] [920]   75-20680
ISBN 0-516-05310-8

Table of Contents

Jean Louis Agassiz

William C. Bond

Agassiz, Jean Louis R. After establishing an international reputation in the 1830s for his studies of the Ice Age, Jean Agassiz became America's most prominent natural scientist by developing new and original programs of study and research. Before arriving in the U.S. in 1846, Agassiz conducted experiments to follow his original belief that much of Europe had been covered by massive glaciers during an ancient Ice Age. Living on top of the Aar glacier in Switzerland, Agassiz drove stakes into the glacier and recorded its movement from the stakes. Other experiments determined the speed and direction of all parts of the glacier. Agassiz later assembled evidence that Ice Age glaciers had at one time covered England and North America.

Born in Switzerland in 1803, Agassiz earned a medical degree from the University of Munich.

But his real interest was in natural science, and he became an expert in classifying fossil fishes. Invited to lecture in the U.S., Agassiz was later appointed to the Lawrence Scientific School at Harvard in 1848 and began collecting animal specimens for his own museum of comparative biology. The museum later became part of the university. Emphasizing the direct study of nature, Agassiz stressed the use of active field trips. In his many writings, he opposed Darwin's theory of evolution, believing instead that many creatures were created in their final form and were not evolved by time and needs. Before he died in 1873, Agassiz stated his belief that "the study of nature is a connection with the Highest Mind. You should never trifle with the laws of nature."

Bond: William C. and George P. Pioneering the use of new instruments to record the positions of stars, William Bond and his son George, the first to use telescopic photography when observing stars, planets, and comets, made significant astronomical discoveries in the 19th century. William, born in Maine, September 9, 1789, had little formal education but made precision ship clocks and navigational instruments at an early age. A constant observer of the skies, he studied astronomy on his own and in 1839 became director of Harvard College's new observatory. George, born near Boston, May 20, 1825, graduated from Harvard, then moved from assistant to head of the observatory after his father died in 1859. He discovered Hyperion, the eighth satellite of Saturn, learned that Saturn's rings were not solid, and wrote a detailed paper, often used by later astronomers, on the Donati comet of 1858. George Bond died in 1865.

Alvan G. Clark   **John W. Draper**   **Josiah Gibbs**

Clark, Alvan G. Nineteenth century astronomer Alvan Clark is credited with the discovery of 16 double stars and won the French Academy of Science's medal for his discovery of the companion star of Sirius. Clark, born in Massachusetts in 1832, became fascinated by telescopes early in his youth. At the age of twenty, he joined his father's optical firm as a lens grinder. The firm's telescopes became known and used by astronomers all over the world.

Draper, John W. Acclaimed for his studies of history and scientific writings, John Draper in the mid-1800s pioneered discoveries in physiology, radiant energy, and photography. Born in England in 1811, Draper immigrated to the U.S. in 1832. While completing his medical degree at the University of Pennsylvania in 1836, he helped explain osmosis, the transfer of oxygen from lung cells to the blood. Joining the faculty of the University of the City of New York, Draper helped found the school's medical college and became its president in 1850. Author of many books on science, he wrote the popular textbook *Human Physiology* in 1856 and published several studies on light, which contained the principle of the later incandescent lamp. Draper also won recognition for his books on the Civil War and his *History of the Intellectual Development of Europe* (1863). He died in New York, January 4, 1882.

Astronomers using Clark's instruments discovered the satellites of Mars and one of the satellites of Jupiter. Clark's greatest achievement was the manufacture of the world's largest refracting (lens) telescope, the 40-inch Yerkes telescope, located at Williams Bay, Wisconsin. Newer and larger telescopes were later made with reflecting mirrors instead of lenses. Clark died June 9, 1897, shortly after delivering the lenses to Wisconsin.

Gibbs, Josiah Willard. Mathematician, physicist, and research scientist Josiah Gibbs in 1876 created a theory of the action of heat on dissimilar substances that became the basis of a new branch of science known as physical chemistry. Born in Connecticut in 1839, Gibbs received his Ph.D. from Yale in 1863. Continuing advanced studies in Europe, he worked with outstanding mathematicians and physicists. Appointed professor of physics at Yale in 1871, Gibbs began his research that pushed the knowledge of thermodynamics to new understanding. His theories made possible the production of new kinds of metals and the discovery of the composition of Portland cement and methods of its manufacture. Gibbs's unique theory, *On The Equilibrium of Heterogeneous Substances* (1876), established him as one of the foremost American theoretical scientists. Gibbs died in Connecticut in 1903.

Asaph Hall

Ferdinand V. Hayden

Hall, Asaph. Working to advance the knowledge of the solar system, astronomer Asaph Hall in 1877 discovered the two satellites which circle the planet Mars. He named them Phobos and Deimos after the sons of the legendary god of war, Mars. Hall wrote more than 500 papers detailing his discoveries. Observing a white spot on the surface of the planet Saturn, he measured the time of Saturn's rotation once around the sun and found it to be 10¾ hours. He also calculated the orbits, distances, and size of several other planets and stars.

Born in Goshen, Connecticut in 1829, Hall worked as a carpenter's apprentice at age 13. He attended Central College in New York in 1854 before enrolling at the University of Michigan in 1856. Leaving after one year, he joined the staff of the Harvard College Observ-atory. Between 1858 and 1862, Hall published several papers on comets and asteroids, winning wide recognition for his work. In 1862 he moved to the U.S. Naval Observatory in Washington, D.C. and in 1863 was named to the observatory's permanent staff as professor of mathematics and astronomy. Hall soon began his research, using the Naval Observatory's 26-inch refractor, the largest telescope then available. He calculated the positions of many stars, comets, satellites, and planets, and in 1877 he surprised the scientific world by observing for the first time the two satellites of Mars. After retiring from the Naval Observatory in 1891, Hall taught astronomy at Harvard and continued to write articles until shortly before his death in Annapolis, Maryland in 1907.

Hayden, Ferdinand Vandeveer. A pioneer geologist and geographer of the western U.S. during the mid-1800s, Ferdinand Hayden conducted explorations that led to formation of the U.S. Geological Survey and creation of Yellowstone National Park in 1879. Born in Massachusetts in 1829, Hayden graduated from Oberlin College in 1850. Three years later, he won a medical degree from Albany Medical College. Interested in geology, he traveled to the South Dakota Badlands in 1853 and during the next six years explored mountainous regions throughout the West and Northwest. After serving as a Union surgeon during the Civil War, he joined the faculty of the University of Pennsylvania, serving until 1872. Hayden conducted explorations of the West (1867-1879), winning recognition as one of the world's leading geologists. He worked as a geologist with the Geological Survey (1879-1886). Hayden died in 1887.

Edward Hitchcock   **Alpheus Hyatt**   **Orange Judd**

Hitchcock, Edward. An investigation by geologist Edward Hitchcock in the early 1800s led to proof that prehistoric dinosaurs once roamed the Connecticut Valley. Earlier, Hitchcock established his reputation as a geologist by leading a geological survey of Massachusetts, the first scientific survey completed of any state. Born in 1793 in Massachusetts, Hitchcock became an educator and clergyman in addition to a scientist. After preaching in Massa-chusetts (1821-25), he was appointed a professor at Amherst and later served as president of the college. In 1840 Hitchcock became the first chairman of the Association of American Geologists and Naturalists and was a strong force in expanding the group to include all scientists. Hitchcock wrote many books and papers on geology and religion, skillfully handling the delicate relationship between the two. Hitchcock died in 1864.

Hyatt, Alpheus. One of America's first important zoologists, Alpheus Hyatt helped found the Woods Hole Marine Biological Laboratory in 1879, which grew to become one of the world's leading centers for the study of undersea life. Born in 1838 in Washington, D.C., Hyatt studied at Harvard under the famous scientist Louis Agassiz, acquiring a lifelong interest in zoology and paleontology, the study of fossil remains of early animal life. He served in the Union army during the Civil War, rising to the rank of captain. After the war he resumed his scientific career, becoming a professor of zoology and paleontology at Massachusetts Institute of Technology. He helped found *American Naturalist,* the nation's first biology magazine and in 1881 was appointed curator, or chief scientist, of the Boston Society of Natural History. Hyatt served as first president of the Woods Hole Laboratory. He died in 1902.

Judd, Orange. Realizing the farmer's need for advanced techniques to grow better crops, Orange Judd, beginning in the 1850s, printed detailed instructions that led the way to greater crop production. His service was the first of its kind in America and was later followed and enlarged by the U.S. Department of Agriculture. Born in 1822 in New York, Judd graduated from Wesleyan University in 1847 and entered Yale's agricultural chemistry program. He joined the *American Agriculturalist* magazine in 1853 and wrote practical articles explaining scientific farming in language an average farmer could understand. Judd purchased the *Agriculturalist* in 1856 and began publishing additional magazines of interest to the farming community. Judd's magazines included *Hearth and Home, Prairie Farmer,* and *Orange Judd Farmer.* Later he established a science hall at Wesleyan. He died in 1892.

Clarence King

Joseph Leidy

King, Clarence. Directing a geological survey along the 40th parallel from eastern Colorado to California between 1867 and 1877, Clarence King paved the way for the first systematic geological survey of the entire United States. The findings of King and other geologists in his corps were published in a seven-volume governmental publication entitled *Report of the Geological Exploration of the Fortieth Parallel.* King's *Systematic Geology* was the first volume of the study, and the entire report was so complete and well organized that Congress in 1878 appointed King director of the newly established United States Geological Survey.

Born in Newport, Rhode Island in 1842, King graduated from Yale University's Sheffield Scientific School in 1862. The following year he traveled to California, crossing the Sierra mountains on foot and later joining a geological group that explored the desert region of southern California. The experience gave King the idea of making a survey along the 40th parallel. He returned to the East and in 1866 influenced Congress to provide funds for the project. Under King's direction, a team of geologists explored an area about 100 miles in width extending along the lines of the 40th parallel. During the survey, King became one of the first geologists to make use of laboratory science to solve many problems relating to earth and its formation. Highly regarded as a leader of scientific explorations, King's most significant contribution was the highly detailed and understandable reports of his survey. He died in Phoenix, Arizona in 1901.

Leidy, Joseph. Through his study of the remains of plants and animals that existed on the American continent millions of years before, zoologist Joseph Leidy established paleontology in the last part of the 1800s as a major science in the U.S. From the fossil samples he studied, Leidy determined that many types of animals had previously existed on the North American continent. Leidy's book *Cretaceous Reptiles of the United States* (1865) was described by many 19th century scientists as the most significant work produced in America on the study of ancient animal life.

Leidy was born in Pennsylvania in 1823 and in 1847 graduated from the University of Pennsylvania, where he was appointed professor of anatomy in 1853. He also served as professor of natural history at Swarthmore College. His studies of the human body were detailed in his book *An Elementary Treatise on Human Anatomy* (1861, revised 1889). For many years the book remained the standard American textbook for medical students. During the Civil War, Leidy served as a surgeon with the Union army. He acquired a broad knowledge of comparative anatomy and after the war pioneered in the study of vertebrate fossils. Leidy argued that the horse had lived on the American continent long before the time of Christopher Columbus. Discovery of older geologic rocks in Wyoming provided the study for Leidy's last major work, *Contributions to the Extinct Vertebrate Fauna of the Western Territories.* He was an original member of the National Academy of Sciences. Leidy died in 1891.

Matthew F. Maury

Maria Mitchell

Maury, Matthew F. A farm boy who became an authority on the science of oceanography, Matthew Maury taught ship captains in the 19th century how to use winds and sea currents for faster ocean trips. He also discovered a prominent deep ridge in the mid-Atlantic Ocean and studied the course of the Gulf Stream. Born in Virginia in 1806, Maury joined the U.S. Navy when he was 19 years old and traveled around the world. A stagecoach accident in 1839 left him lame and unfit for further sea duty. Appointed superintendent of the Naval Observatory and Hydrographic Office in 1842, Maury began to study ocean currents and winds over the surface of the sea. He issued new navigation charts for the Atlantic, Pacific, and Indian oceans which enabled ship captains to reduce the sailing time for their voyages.

Maury organized an international conference in 1853 which began an exchange of oceanographic information. From information assembled at the conference, he wrote *The Physical Geography of the Sea* (1855), which is credited as the first modern textbook on oceanography. When Virginia seceded from the Union during the Civil War, Maury resigned from the United States Navy to become a Confederate navy commander and was sent to England to obtain naval supplies. At the conclusion of the war, Maury went into voluntary exile in Mexico. He traveled to England in 1866 and finally returned to the U.S. in 1868 to become a professor at the Virginia Military Institute. Maury died in 1873.

Mitchell, Maria. One of America's first woman scientists, Maria Mitchell in 1847 discovered a previously unknown comet and later became the first woman professor of astronomy. Born in 1818 in Massachusetts, she began as a young girl helping her father with his hobby of astronomy. Excelling in mathematics in school, she soon advanced beyond her teacher's knowledge and began to study on her own. Appointed town librarian, she used the opportunity to read books on astronomy and mathematics. Exploring the sky with her father's telescope one evening in October 1847, she sighted a comet never before observed. The comet discovery won her many honors, including a gold medal from the king of Denmark. In 1861 she was made the first professor of astronomy at Vassar College. She died in 1899, and in 1922 she was elected to the Hall of Fame of New York University.

Simon Newcomb   **Edward Orton**   **Alpheus S. Packard**

Newcomb, Simon. The monumental task of determining the positions of stars, finding the mass and distance of the sun, the motion of the moon, and the masses and orbits of the planets and their satellites was undertaken by astronomer Simon Newcomb in the late 19th century. By showing that planet orbits never intersected, Newcomb also disproved the theory that minor planets originated from a larger planet. Born in Nova Scotia in 1835, he moved as a young man to Washington, D.C. Encouraged by Joseph Henry of the Smithsonian Institution, Newcomb graduated from Harvard in 1858 and became a mathematical astronomer at the Naval Observatory in 1861. In 1877 he became superintendent of the *American Ephemeris and Nautical Almanac*. Much of his system of astronomical constants was adopted by an international conference in Paris in 1896. Newcomb died in 1909.

Orton, Edward. A pioneer 19th century conservationist, geologist Edward Orton was one of the first Americans to express concern over the depletion of natural resources. As state geologist of Ohio from 1882 to 1889, Orton pointed out essential conditions for the accumulation of clay, coal, oil, and gas in the earth's crust and warned of their probable exhaustion through wasteful uses and mining methods. Born the son of a minister in 1829 in New York, Orton graduated from Hamilton College in 1848 and was ordained by the Delaware Presbytery in 1856. His interests in geology and conservation developed during his 20s. He taught natural history from 1856 until 1872, when he became president of Antioch College. As head geologist of Ohio, he completed a survey in 1882 of that state's mineral resources and stressed the economic importance of conservation. He died in 1899.

Packard, Alpheus Spring. A noted entomologist, author, and teacher, Alpheus Packard wrote two of the most comprehensive works on the study of insects during the late 19th century. His *Guide to the Study of Insects* was used as a reference in many colleges and universities and earned Packard election to the National Academy of Sciences in 1872. Packard's *Text-Book of Entomology* deals with the study of structure, organs, development, and changes of insects. Packard was born in 1839 in Maine, received his M.D. in 1861, and assisted in the Maine Geological Survey, documenting the age of rocks by examining fossils in the Fish River region. He served as curator of both the Essex Institute and the Peabody Academy of Science. Packard was co-founder and editor of the *American Naturalist*. He served as a professor at Brown University from 1878 until his death in 1905.

Benjamin Peirce   **John K. Rees**   **Edmund Ruffin**

Peirce, Benjamin. A leading mathematician of the 1800s, Benjamin Peirce developed theories of probability—the likelihood of events—and computed orbits of planets. He won world fame for calculating variations in the movements of Uranus and Neptune. As superintendent of the U.S. Coast and Geodetic Survey in 1867, he began an effort to map the entire nation. Born in 1809 in Massachusetts, Peirce was attracted to mathematics by Nathaniel Bowditch. Graduating from Harvard in 1829, Peirce joined the faculty there and served as a professor of mathematics and astronomy from 1833 to 1880. Peirce wrote many textbooks on mathematics. He helped found the Harvard Observatory and was one of fifty incorporators of the National Academy of Sciences in 1863. Peirce was also a president of the American Association for the Advancement of Science. He died in 1880.

Rees, John K. Serving as secretary of the American Metrological Society from 1882 to 1896, astronomer John Rees helped establish the system of standard time that became the official time used throughout the United States. Rees also aided in the improvement of techniques used in photographing stars. Born in 1851 in New York, Rees graduated from Columbia College in 1872 and from the Columbia School of Mines in 1875. Six years later he was appointed director of the Columbia Observatory and instructor in practical astronomy and geodesy (study of the size and shape of the earth). During the 1890s, Rees conducted studies that resulted in improved methods of measuring distances of lengths influenced by the curvature of the earth. Honored at the Paris Exposition of 1900, he helped establish Columbia's summer school of geodesy. Rees died in 1907.

Ruffin, Edmund. A pioneer agriculturist whose discoveries in 1818 enabled farmers to restore fertility to their land, Edmund Ruffin revolutionized farming methods throughout the world. Born in 1794 in Virginia, Ruffin attended the College of William and Mary before serving in the War of 1812. Upon returning to Virginia, he discovered that the soil of many farms had been weakened by years of one-crop cultivation. Experimenting with marl—earth containing calcium and magnesium carbonates—before fertilizing and planting different crops each year, Ruffin restored the fertility to his land. He published his findings in *An Essay on Calcareous Manures* (1832). He established experimental farms and published books and periodicals. An ardent secessionist, Ruffin was given the honor of firing the first shot against Fort Sumter in 1861. Ruffin ended his own life in 1865.

Benjamin Silliman   George M. Sternberg   John Torrey

Silliman, Benjamin. Considered one of America's outstanding men of science in the first half of the 19th century, Benjamin Silliman became Yale College's first professor of chemistry and natural history in 1802 and helped found the National Academy of Sciences in 1863. Born in Connecticut in 1779, Silliman graduated from Yale at 17. He studied in Europe, and after his appointment as professor at Yale in 1802, his scientific lectures, including many on mineral-ogy and geology, became so popular that they were opened to the public. Silliman was a leader in the establishment of the Yale Medical School in 1813 and was instrumental in founding in 1847 the Department of Philosophy and Arts that later became the Sheffield Scientific School. In 1818 he published one of science's leading journals, the *American Journal of Science and Arts*, and served as editor. Silliman served at Yale for over 50 years and died in 1864.

Sternberg, George M. A pioneer in the study of bacteria, George Sternberg, an army surgeon, promoted medical research programs in the late 19th century that resulted in the conquest of yellow fever. Born in New York in 1838, Sternberg obtained a medical degree in 1860 from the College of Physicians and Surgeons in New York City. An army surgeon during the Civil War, he served in several army hospitals. After the war, Sternberg studied the causes of yellow fever and other diseases at the same time French scientist Louis Pasteur announced an identical discovery. Sternberg announced the discovery in 1881 of pneumococcus, the bacterial agent causing pneumonia. A pioneer in the methods of disinfection, Sternberg prevented an epidemic of cholera from spreading in New York in 1892 after sailors were found to be carrying the disease. Sternberg died in Washington, D.C. in 1915.

Torrey, John. One of the leading 19th century botanists in the U.S., John Torrey wrote much of the early book, *Flora of North America* (1838-43), that remained a leading authority on American plants for more than 100 years. Torrey was born in 1796 in New York and studied medicine. He received his M.D. in 1818 from the College of Physicians and Surgeons. As a botanist, his thorough investigations won him a worldwide reputation, and he soon was receiving complete plant collections for study. Torrey published his first botanical work in 1823, *A Flora of the Northern and Middle Sections of the United States*. Appointed professor at the United States Military Academy in 1824, he was selected state botanist of New York in 1836 and completed *Flora of the State of New York* (2 vols., 1843). Appointed U.S. assayer in 1853, Torrey was one of the founders of the National Academy of Sciences. He died in 1873.

Luther Burbank

Herbert H. Dow

Burbank, Luther. Breeding flowers and vegetables in the late 19th and early 20th centuries, Luther Burbank developed 90 new varieties of vegetables and 113 new types of fruit. "I shall be content," Burbank said, "if because of me there shall be better fruits and fairer flowers." Born in Massachusetts in 1849, Burbank grew up on a farm and attended local schools. After graduating from Lancaster Academy at the age of 19, he began his lifework of experiments in plant breeding.

Burbank's first success was the Burbank Potato (1873). Moving to California in 1875, he concentrated on producing improved varieties of cultivated plants, raising over a million plants each year for his experiments. The results made Burbank's "little garden" famous all over the world. Tastier vegetables were discovered which included peas, corn, tomatoes, squash, and asparagus. Sweeter and fleshier fruits were bred—prunes, plums, apples, peaches, and nectarines. One of Burbank's unique creations was the thornless edible Opuntia Cactus which took 16 years to develop and was used to feed cattle in dry areas. Burbank produced many new roses, callas, poppies, daisies, including the popular Shasta, and a wax myrtle. His special talent was his ability to pick the one seedling out of many that would produce a better plant. Burbank's invaluable scientific writings include *Luther Burbank, His Methods and Discoveries* (1914-15) and *How Plants Are Trained to Work For Man* (1921). While working on his autobiography, Burbank died in Santa Rosa, California in 1926.

Dow, Herbert H. By combining his knowledge of chemistry with a vivid imagination, Herbert Dow in the 1890s began producing formulas that resulted in hundreds of new products for use in homes, farms, and industry. Born in Ontario, Canada in 1866, he received a science degree from the Case School in Cleveland in 1888. His thesis on brines and his further research became the foundation of a new chemical industry. By forcing air through brine, Dow developed a process to obtain bromine for use in fumigants, dyes, and photographic chemicals. His method of processing did not require evaporation of brine to the point where it became common salt. A direct current generator was needed and when this was installed in 1892, Dow owned the first electrochemical plant in the United States.

Convinced that an idea that appeared workable should be pursued until successful, Dow made further experiments with brine to discover many possible uses for the fluid. He produced chlorine for use in many ways, including purification of water and as a disinfectant. Bleaching powder also was obtained from chlorine and Dow's interest in gardening led him to develop insecticides from the same source. Magnesium metal was also produced and many alloys developed from it were called Dowmetal. Dow also produced synthetic indigos for dyes, anilines for use in rubber and varnishes, and phenols for plastics and resins. He was awarded 65 patents for chemical processes and received the Perkin medal from the Society of Chemical Industry. He died in 1930.

Clarence E. Dutton   **Jacques Loeb**   **Percival Lowell**

Dutton, Clarence E. A field geologist during the late 1800s, Clarence Dutton became the first scientist to suggest that radioactivity beneath the earth's crust could help cause volcanic eruptions. Born in Connecticut in 1841, Dutton graduated from Yale in 1860. Commissioned an officer in the Union army during the Civil War, he served until 1875, then joined the U.S. Geological Survey. For the next ten years, Dutton traveled throughout the western states studying the earth's geologic structure. He developed methods to help determine the origins of earthquakes and the speed of their shock waves. Dutton also proposed the theory (isostasy) that huge areas of rock rise or fall in the earth's crust, creating continents and ocean floors. In 1906 he suggested that radioactivity might slowly heat up local areas of the earth's crust, thus setting off volcanic action. Dutton died in New Jersey in 1912.

Loeb, Jacques. In the late 19th century, biologist Jacques Loeb studied the reactions of plant life to such influences as light, water, and gravity. This led him to theorize that these reactions, called tropisms, might also influence the freedom of will of ordinary human actions. Loeb's ideas created a sensation and had some effect on philosophy and psychology during that period. Born in Germany in 1859, Loeb received an M.D. from the University of Strassburg in 1884 and in 1891 joined the faculty of the University of Chicago. He attracted scientific attention in 1899 when he changed environmental conditions surrounding an unfertilized sea urchin egg and caused it to mature without a male sex cell. Loeb moved to the University of California in 1902 and to the Rockefeller Institute for Medical Research in New York in 1910. He founded the *Journal of General Physiology*. Loeb died in 1924.

Lowell, Percival. A pioneer astronomer and founder in 1894 of the Lowell Observatory, Percival Lowell made significant studies of planets which advanced the scientific knowledge of outer space. Born in Boston in 1855, Lowell graduated from Harvard University in 1876. Returning from travel in the Orient, he chose a site in Arizona to begin observing the planets. Lowell believed that the canals sighted on Mars had been constructed by its inhabitants to halt the disappearance of water. In 1905 he organized a systematic search by his staff for a planet that he believed was causing the wobbling of the planet Uranus. The search ended in 1930 with the discovery of the planet Pluto. Lowell made many discoveries, including new divisions of rings on the planet Saturn and valuable data on the solar system. He wrote many books on astronomy, including *Mars and its Canals* (1906). Lowell died in 1916.

Albert Michelson

Thomas Hunt Morgan

Michelson, Albert. Discovering in an 1887 experiment that the speed of light never changes regardless of the motion of either the source or the observer, Albert Michelson developed a basic physical theory and in 1907 became the first American to win a Nobel Prize in the sciences. Working in collaboration with Edward W. Morley, he disproved the theory that a light-carrying "ether" exists in space, and that the earth travels through the motionless ether. Although light sent in the direction the earth is traveling should move faster than light sent out at right angles to the earth, Michelson and Morley proved that the speed of light remains the same regardless of the direction of the beam. Accepting Michelson's discovery as completely accurate, Albert Einstein announced in 1905 his theory of relativity, which began with the assumption that the speed of light remains constant.

Born in 1852 in what is now Poland, Michelson came to America with his parents in 1854 and later settled in San Francisco. Obtaining an appointment to the U.S. Naval Academy, he graduated in 1873 and in 1875-79 served as a physics instructor at the school. After studying light and optics abroad, he became a professor of physics at the Case School of Applied Science in 1883 and was named head of the University of Chicago's physics department in 1892. In 1881 he invented the interferometer, which he used to measure the speed of light and disprove the ether theory. In 1920 he made the first reliable measurement of a star's diameter. Michelson died in 1931.

Morgan, Thomas Hunt. By discovering that chromosomes—substances found in plant and animal cells—contain the carriers of hereditary characteristics (characteristics passed from parents to their offspring), biologist Thomas Hunt Morgan provided the basis for the science of genetics—the study of heredity. For his work, Morgan received the 1933 Nobel Prize in medicine and physiology. By the early 1900s, Morgan and many other scientists believed that chromosomes were connected with heredity. But they wondered why there were only a few chromosomes in the cells of each living thing, while there were a great many inherited (acquired from parents) characteristics. Morgan began his experiments in 1907 using fruit flies, which were suitable for his studies because they multiply rapidly and their cells have only four pairs of chromosomes. His experiments established that chromosomes contain large numbers of tiny, individual units, called genes, which actually carry the inherited characteristics from one generation to the next.

Morgan was born in Kentucky in 1866. He obtained his Ph.D. from Johns Hopkins University in 1890 and became a professor of biology at Bryn Mawr College in 1891, a post he held until 1904, when he joined the faculty of Columbia University. In 1928 he was named director of biological sciences at the California Institute of Technology. Morgan's book, *The Theory of the Gene* (1926), is considered to have established genetics as a distinct science and to have laid the foundation for modern molecular biology. Morgan died in 1945.

Edward L. Nichols   William Hallock Park   Edward C. Pickering

Nichols, Edward L. Considered one of the outstanding pioneers in physics, Edward Nichols beginning in the late 1800s stimulated the development of the science through his teachings, research, and writings. Born in England in 1854 to American parents, Nichols graduated from Cornell in 1875 and spent four years in Europe studying with German scientists. After returning to America, he assisted Thomas Edison in 1880 with his research on incandescent light.

Nichols wrote more than 200 papers, many of them detailing his experiments on aspects of light. From 1887 until 1919, he served as chairman of the Department of Physics at Cornell University. At his retirement, his former students headed physics departments at 35 American colleges. He founded the first American journal of physics, the *Physical Review*, in 1893 and edited it for twenty years. Nichols died in West Palm Beach, Florida in 1937.

Park, William Hallock. Determined to stamp out one of the world's dread diseases, bacteriologist William Park played a leading role in practically eliminating diphtheria as a cause of death in the 1930s. Born in 1863 in New York City, Park gained his medical degree in 1886 at Columbia University's College of Physicians and Surgeons. He began diphtheria research in 1890 and in 1893 was placed in charge of diphtheria work at New York City's Board of Health diagnostic laboratory. After European scientists discovered medicines to treat and prevent diphtheria, Park improved on them, and in 1920 he set up a city-wide immunization program that came to be followed all over the world. Park also helped bring about compulsory pasteurization of milk. A professor of preventive medicine at Bellevue Hospital's Medical College from 1933 to 1937, Park died in 1939.

Pickering, Edward C. As director of the Harvard Observatory from 1877 to 1919, physicist Edward Pickering developed the star classification system now in use throughout the world. Born in 1846 in Massachusetts, Pickering graduated from Harvard University in 1865. He was named professor of physics at Massachusetts Institute of Technology in 1868. Until he became director of the Harvard Observatory in 1877, astronomy had been a matter of locating stars and planets. Pickering developed a "new astronomy" that sought to discover the evolution and structure of stars. Using photography, he measured the intensity of light from 80,000 stars, establishing their distance and stage of life. He took 300,000 photographs of the night sky and plotted the movement of stars by comparing pictures taken over a period of time. Twice winner of the Royal Astronomical Society's gold medal, he died in 1919.

Michael Pupin

Theodore W. Richards

Pupin, Michael. Immigrating to the U.S. at age 15, Michael Pupin became a prominent physicist, winning 34 patents for his inventions, and after writing his autobiography *From Immigrant to Inventor* he was awarded a 1924 Pulitzer Prize. Pupin believed America to be a land of opportunity and described his own career as evidence. Born in 1858 in Hungary, Pupin arrived in the U.S. in 1873 and was soon granted a scholarship to continue his studies. He graduated in 1883 from Columbia University and received his Ph.D. from the University of Berlin in 1889. After returning to the U.S., Pupin was appointed professor at Columbia.

Among Pupin's major inventions was a system that would help transmit sound over long-distance wires. Following a method used by Serbian herdsmen to transmit messages by tapping codes on a knife driven into the earth, Pupin concluded that sound carries farther over longer distances when passed through earth than through air. To produce the effect electrically on a telephone line, he installed induction coils every four or five miles along the wire and found that sound could be transmitted over long-distance lines when boosted by the induction coils. Pupin produced the first x-ray photograph in the U.S. in 1896 and later invented the fluoroscope, a device that produces an image when exposed by x-rays. The medical profession became one of the major users of Pupin's fluoroscope for diagnostic purposes, since it provided a picture-image of internal organs. Pupin continued to teach at Columbia until 1931 and died in 1935.

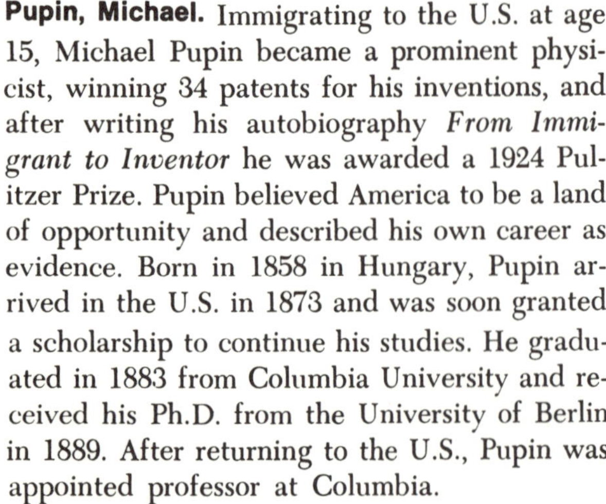

Richards, Theodore W. For developing chemistry into a precise science and supervising accurate measurements of the atomic weights of 60 chemical elements, Theodore Richards won the 1914 Nobel Prize for chemistry. To eliminate the slightest errors of measurement, Richards devised new experimental tools: a quartz weighing apparatus, a "bottling process" to keep moisture from polluting his samples, and a device to measure particles suspended in liquid. By his studies on lead in 1913, he was able to confirm chemically the existence of isotopes—atoms with whole-numbered weights that occur in nature mixed together in the same element. He later studied the heat properties of solids and their compressibility. Richards was born in Pennsylvania in 1868 and received his doctorate at Harvard University in 1888. After study in Europe, Richards taught chemistry at Harvard until his death in Massachusetts in 1928.

Robert Ridgway   **George W. Ritchey**   **Harry L. Russell**

Ridgway, Robert. America's leading expert in the study of bird life in the late 1800s, Robert Ridgway helped found the American Ornithologists' Union in 1833. He wrote many detailed and scholarly books on birds, including the eight-volume *Birds of North and Middle America*. This work is considered one of the most outstanding systematic studies on birds ever compiled, and it received recognition throughout the world. Born in Illinois in 1850, Ridgway joined an expedition which charted bird life in Utah, Nevada, and Wyoming in 1867. He was named curator of birds at the United States National Museum in 1880 and served in that position for nearly half a century. After expeditions to Florida and Alaska in the 1890s, he purchased property in Olney, Illinois which he developed into a bird sanctuary. The preserve was maintained as a memorial to Ridgway after his death in 1929.

Ritchey, George W. One of America's leading astronomers from 1896 to 1945, George Ritchey designed and built huge telescopes that enabled scientists to unlock mysteries of the universe. Born in Ohio in 1864, Ritchey attended the University of Cincinnati. In 1896 he joined the staff of Yerkes Observatory in Wisconsin and in 1899 was named superintendent of instrument construction. Moving to the Carnegie Institution's Mt. Wilson Observatory in 1905, he designed and built its 60-inch and 100-inch reflecting telescopes. Coinventor of an aplanatic reflecting telescope that corrects the blurred and warped images caused by spherical surfaces, Ritchey became director of the astrophotographic laboratory at the Paris Observatory, serving from 1924 to 1930. After returning to the U.S., he designed and constructed a 40-inch reflecting telescope for the Naval Observatory in Washington. Ritchey died in 1945.

Russell, Harry L. A pioneer in developing a medical test for detecting tuberculosis in dairy herds, bacteriologist Harry Russell made many notable contributions to dairy farming during the first half of the 20th century. His discoveries included a cold-curing process that produced cheese of a uniformly high quality and was quickly adopted by dairymen all over the world. Born in Wisconsin in 1866, Russell received his Ph.D. from the University of Wisconsin in 1890 and later studied in Berlin and the Pasteur Institute in Paris. In 1893 he was appointed assistant professor of bacteriology at Wisconsin, rising to full professor in 1897. He was appointed dean of the College of Agriculture at the University of Wisconsin in 1907. He resigned in 1930 to direct a foundation organized to patent the scientific discoveries developed at the university and to use the proceeds for further research. Russell died in 1954.

Charles de Medicis Sajous

Daniel Elmer Salmon

Sajous, Charles de Medicis. A doctor and medical researcher in the late 1800s and early 1900s, Charles Sajous made a significant contribution to medicine by his study of glands and their role in fighting disease. He was one of the most productive writers and editors of medical literature at the turn of the century. His major work on glands was published in two volumes, *Internal Secretions and the Principles of Medicine* (1903-07). Sajous was born at sea during a voyage by his parents from Italy to France in 1852. When he was two his father died, and after his mother married Charles Sajous, the boy assumed the name of his stepfather. He traveled to the U.S. to study medicine at the University of California and at Jefferson Medical College in Philadelphia. After graduation and a term as resident physician at a Philadelphia hospital, he began practicing medicine while serving as professor of anatomy and physiology at the Wagner Free Institute of Science and at Jefferson Medical College.

Interested in the new medical field of endocrinology, the study of glands, Sajous went abroad in 1891 to study in France and Germany. On his return to America in 1897, he was appointed professor and dean of the Medico-Chirurgical College in Philadelphia. He edited the *Annual of the Universal Medical Sciences* and contributed many articles on his own studies. He later edited the *Annual and Analytical Cyclopaedia of Practical Medicine.* In 1909 he joined the faculty of Temple University and became a professor at the University of Pennsylvania in 1921. Sajous died in 1929.

Salmon, Daniel Elmer. A pioneer in scientific research on diseases of animals, Daniel Salmon in 1883 organized and became the first chief of the Bureau of Animal Industry in the U.S. Department of Agriculture. He directed research and field testing that brought under control diseases that threatened cattle, poultry, pigs, and sheep in the United States. Salmon was responsible for organizing U.S. meat inspection, quarantines for imported livestock, and a system for inspecting exported cattle. He also served as president of both the American Public Health Association and the Veterinary Medical Association.

Salmon was born in New Jersey in 1850, enrolled in the first freshman class at Cornell in 1868, graduated in 1872 as a bachelor of veterinary science, and received a degree of doctor of veterinary medicine in 1876. A year later he began a special study of diseases of pigs and in 1879 accepted an assignment from the U.S. Department of Agriculture to study Texas fever affecting cattle. Besides his work on Texas fever, he succeeded in virtually eliminating contagious pleuropneumonia in cattle. In 1883 he was asked to organize the veterinary division that became the Bureau of Animal Industry. An able administrator, Salmon took time from his duties to write nearly 100 articles covering a large section of veterinary research. He traveled to Uruguay in 1906 to organize the veterinary department of the University of Montevideo, and after his return he began the production of medical serums for use by veterinarians. Salmon died in 1914.

Thomas J. J. See

Agustin Stahl

See, Thomas J. J. By examining more than 200,000 fixed stars, astronomer Thomas See recorded many significant observations about stars and planets and discovered more than 600 double stars. He organized the department of astronomy at the University of Chicago in 1892 and helped establish the Yerkes Observatory in Lake Geneva, Wisconsin two years later. Born in 1866 in Missouri, See graduated from the University of Missouri in 1889, winning a medal for his studies on double stars. After receiving a Ph.D. from the University of Berlin in 1892, he was appointed director of the University of Chicago's department of astronomy. See began a survey for the Lowell Observatory in Arizona in 1896 and studied double stars and nebulae.

Appointed professor of mathematics in 1899 for the U.S. Navy by President McKinley, he served for the next three years at the Naval Observatory in Washington, D.C. See observed double stars and satellites with a 26-inch telescope and took measurements of satellites and planets by both day and night. After duty at the Naval Academy in 1902-03, he was named director of the Naval Observatory at Mare Island, California, where he studied the nature of heavenly bodies and origin of the solar system. He also did extensive research on gravitation and land and water hemispheres of the earth. See wrote several books, including *Researches on the Evolution of the Solar System* in 1896, *Capture Theory of Cosmical Evolution* in 1910, and *Eighth and Ninth Mathematical Memoirs on the New Theory of Aether* (1925). See died in Oakland, California in 1962.

Stahl, Agustin. Combining his skills as a medical doctor and nature scientist in the late 1800s, Agustin Stahl studied diseases of sugar cane plants and also wrote the first history of the early Indians of Puerto Rico. His book *The Island Indians* (1890) is an extensive study of how the Indians lived and their tribal customs. He also published his studies of the fertility of Puerto Rican women. He spent years at an island agricultural station, studying the many diseases that attack the sugar cane plant, and summarized his research and discoveries in a two-volume book set. His later findings were completed by Carlos Chadron.

Stahl was born in Aguadilla, Puerto Rico in 1842 and, after attending schools on the island, studied at the University of Wurzburg in Germany. He graduated as a medical surgeon from the University of Prague in 1864. Stahl also received a degree in science in Barcelona, Spain. He returned to the Puerto Rican islands and, after practicing medicine in various hospitals, established a permanent residence and practice in Bayamon. A keen observer of nature, Stahl gradually reduced his medical practice and concentrated his studies on plants and archaeology. He became professor of natural history at the Institute of Secondary Education in San Juan in 1874. Under his direction, a natural history museum was organized where 2,300 species of botanical specimens, which he had classified and sketched, were placed on display. Later, the collection was purchased by a New Orleans scientific society. Stahl was writing a study of Puerto Rican flowers when he died in 1917.

Charles Steinmetz

Steinmetz, Charles. One of the outstanding scientists and inventors in the United States in the early 1900s, electrical engineer Charles Steinmetz discovered a new magnetic law and was the first to calculate alternating current. Awarded more than 200 patents, including improvements on generators, motors, transformers, and regulators, Steinmetz was a leading force in transferring the theories of science into practical machines and devices. He also made new investigations of lightning that resulted in improved safety and protection.

Steinmetz was born in Breslau, Germany in 1865 and enrolled at the University of Breslau in 1883. Editor of a student Socialist newspaper, his activities led Steinmetz into difficulty with the government authorities, and he was forced to flee Germany in 1888. Although he had already completed a thesis for his doctor's degree, he left Germany without receiving the award. He sailed to the United States in 1889 and soon found employment as a draftsman for an electrical machinery manufacturer. Steinmetz quickly adjusted to the U.S. and joined the American Institute of Electrical Engineers. In 1892 the firm he worked for was absorbed by a large electric company, and he was appointed consulting engineer. He held that position for the next thirty years.

Steinmetz designed an alternating current commutator motor and found it necessary to measure optional losses of efficiency due to alternating magnetism, called hysteresis. Although the law governing power loss was unknown, Steinmetz proved its existence and simplified its application. To enable engineers and scientists to follow his new methods and discoveries, Steinmetz wrote several textbooks, including *Theoretical Elements of Electrical Engineering* (1901) and *Engineering Mathematics* (1911). The books became widely read and helped in the understanding of Steinmetz's symbolic method, which later became universally accepted in calculating alternating current. Steinmetz's investigation of lightning phenomena was first published in 1907. From this study, he later developed lightning arrestors for the protection of power transmission lines. As a result of his earlier work, Steinmetz observed the first man-made lightning in a laboratory.

He served a professorship at Union College from 1902 until 1923 and frequently lectured to electrical engineers throughout the U.S. He was appointed president of the American Institute of Electrical Engineers in 1901. Steinmetz died in New York in 1923.

Jokichi Takamine   **David Todd**   **Warren Upham**

Takamine, Jokichi. By his significant discovery in 1901 of the first glandular hormone, a bodily produced chemical that stimulates other organs, chemist Jokichi Takamine opened a new understanding of the functions of the body. Takamine's hormone, later labeled adrenalin, became the first major medical advance of the 20th century. Born in Japan in 1854, Takamine grew up when Japanese schools were beginning to teach modern science. He graduated as a chemical engineer from the Japanese Imperial University in 1879, and seeking to help farmers grow more crops, he started production of chemical fertilizer. After visiting the United States in 1885, he decided to settle permanently in the U.S. In addition to his discovery of adrenalin, Takamine experimented with chemicals for industrial use. He isolated an enzyme he named Takadiastase, which proved useful in medicine. Takamine died in 1922.

Todd, David. Organizer of twelve research trips between 1878 and 1914 to observe and photograph the sun as it blacked out in space, astronomer David Todd devised the first automatic photographic apparatus for taking pictures of the sun during an eclipse. Todd's photographic techniques were studied by Thomas Edison and were believed to influence Edison's motion pictures. Todd was born in New York in 1855 and received a master's degree at Amherst College in 1878. He worked as an astronomer for the U.S. Naval Observatory until 1881, when he returned to Amherst as director of the observatory. Todd was appointed professor of astronomy at Amherst in 1892, a position he held throughout his life. His textbook *New Astronomy* was printed in twenty-five editions. In 1925, Todd, with the aid of the U.S. Army Air Service, photographed the first aerial pictures of the solar corona. He died in 1939.

Upham, Warren. An authority on postglacial land formation who published more than 200 scientific papers on the organized structure of the earth, geologist Warren Upham made further studies in history and archaeology in the early 1900s and became convinced that man inhabited the region beyond the ice edge of the last glacier. Upham's paper "The Glacial Lake Agassiz," published in 1896, described postglacial land formation in the Lake Winnipeg area. He believed that a vast, ancient lake existed at one time, and when the lake shrank in size, it revealed shore features that became Lake Winnipeg. Born in 1850 in New Hampshire, Upham graduated from Dartmouth in 1871 and was affiliated with the U.S. Geological Survey until 1895. His studies in geology led him into many fields in history and archaeology. He was a leading editor of *Minnesota in Three Centuries*, published in 1908. Upham died in 1934.

Roger Adams   **Walter Baade**   **Georg von Bekesy**

Adams, Roger. By breaking down the chemical structure of substances such as alkali solutions, fatty acids, and drugs, organic chemist Roger Adams in the early 1900s was able to develop new and useful products, including a cottonseed oil for cooking and a painkilling drug to replace cocaine. Born in Boston, Massachusetts in 1889, Adams received his Ph.D. from Harvard in 1912. Joining the faculty at the University of Illinois, Adams was named chairman of the department of chemistry in 1926. While serving in the chemical warfare division during two world wars, he developed a sneezing gas called Adamsite. Winner of the 1947 Priestly Medal, the highest award given in American chemistry, Adams also served as president of the American Association for the Advancement of Science. He later became one of the first scientists to experiment with the effects of marijuana. Adams died in 1971.

Baade, Walter. The universe was estimated to be twenty times larger than previously believed following the discovery by Walter Baade in 1942 that two different classes of stars existed instead of one. Before, only bluish stars had been seen in the arms of galaxies. Baade's data changed the age of the universe from two to six billion years, and he proved that the earth's Milky Way is a galaxy of average size and not the biggest as thought. Born in 1893 in Germany, Baade received his Ph.D. from Gottingen University in 1919 and immigrated to the U.S. in 1931. Using the 100-inch telescope at Mount Wilson, California, Baade found reddish stars near the interior of the Andromeda galaxy. The blue-whites, or young outer stars, he called Population I and the red inner stars Population II. Later, Baade used a 200-inch telescope to continue his investigation of how stars are formed. He died in 1958.

Békésy, Georg von. By explaining how the ear sends sounds to the brain, Georg von Békésy in 1961 became the first physicist to win the Nobel Prize for physiology and medicine. Born in Hungary in 1899, Békésy earned his Ph.D. from the University of Budapest. He began experimenting with acoustics, the science of sound, in 1923 and worked in communications research for 23 years. Moving to the U.S. in 1947, he joined the Psycho-acoustic Laboratory at Harvard. By constructing a mechanical model of the ear, he discovered that the eardrum sends vibrations through the coiled nerve cells of the cochlea, located in the inner ear. When vibrations strike the cochlea, they are changed into electrical impulses that are sent to the brain, which interprets the impulses for loudness, pitch and quality. He also invented diagnostic instruments which improved treatment for ear diseases. Békésy died in 1972.

Bertram Boltwood   **Percy Williams Bridgman**   **Wallace Hume Carothers**

Boltwood, Bertram B. After discovering in 1904 that a radioactive series is composed of related radioactive elements, physicist and chemist Bertram Boltwood helped science open new frontiers in physics and geology. His discovery revealed that a new element is formed after elements release atoms over a long period of time. Uranium, as an example, eventually changes into the stable element lead. By measuring the amount of lead present in uranium ores, Boltwood believed geologists could determine the number of years required for the uranium to change form and thereby estimate the age of each stage in the earth's crust. Boltwood's work also proved helpful to later researchers in nuclear physics. Born in 1870 in Massachusetts, Boltwood earned his Ph.D. in 1897 at Yale, where he did most of his later research. Working under extreme pressure most of his career, Boltwood took his life in 1927.

Bridgman, Percy Williams. Experimenting with the effects of tremendous pressures on various substances, Percy Bridgman won the 1946 Nobel Prize in physics for developing equipment which could exert pressures of several million pounds per square inch. In 1955 Bridgman's work guided the research team which created the first man-made diamond. His experiments determined the physical properties of various substances and helped explain geological processes below the earth's crust. Born in 1882 in Massachusetts, Bridgman received his Ph.D. in 1908 from Harvard, where he taught until his retirement. A supporter of the scientific philosophy called operationalism, Bridgman stressed the importance of defining the physical properties of matter by the functions they perform. His books include *The Nature of Physical Theory* (1938) and *Reflections of a Physicist* (1950). Bridgman took his life in 1961.

Carothers, Wallace Hume. By controlling the combining of molecules into long chains called polymers, research chemist Wallace Carothers in 1930 confirmed the theory that the molecules of carbon compounds could be chemically rearranged to produce clothlike, man-made fibers. Using raw material obtained from coal, other research scientists applied Carothers's discovery to the production of nylon thread that helped revolutionize the textile and other industries. Earlier, in collaboration with Father Julius A. Nieuwland, Carothers developed the synthetic rubber, neoprene. Born in 1896 in Iowa, Carothers earned a doctor's degree in chemistry at the University of Illinois in 1924 and became an industrial chemist. The popularity of Carothers' nylon led to other manufactured fibers for consumer and industrial use. Depressed and in ill health, Carothers took his life in Philadelphia in 1937.

George Washington Carver

Carver, George Washington. Black agricultural chemist George Washington Carver made pioneer discoveries in the early 1900s that led to major changes in the farm economy of the southern states. With the boll weevil attacking cotton fields in 1914 and the tobacco crop failing, Carver traveled through the South explaining to black and white farmers that rotation of such crops as peanuts, soybeans, and sweet potatoes would be profitable and also renew the tired soil. Carver taught farmers the methods of growing these crops. He built a demonstration wagon that he called "my mobile school" to reach farmers in remote areas. To provide markets, he invented many by-products of the harvest, including dyes, ink, soap, cheese, milk substitutes, plastics, paper, synthetic rubber, flour and breakfast food. Carver's method of rotating crops instead of depending on only one or two, brought new security to farmers and new eating habits to the American people.

Carver, born in Missouri about 1860, was kidnaped as an infant. The slaveholder who had owned his mother bought back Carver with a racehorse worth $300. Despite lack of money, Carver was determined to obtain an education. Working as a farmhand to attend a one-room school when possible, Carver was in his twenties when he graduated from high school. The first black student at Simpson College in Iowa, he earned a B.S. degree at the age of thirty. Receiving his M.S. degree from Iowa State College of Agriculture, he became the first black faculty member there. Booker T. Washington in 1896 invited Carver to join the staff of the Tuskegee Institute in Alabama as director of the Department of Agricultural Research. Although urged by both Thomas Edison and Henry Ford to work with them in the early 1900s, Carver preferred to remain in his small laboratory at Tuskegee for the rest of his life. He also served from 1935 as collaborator of the Bureau of Plant Industry, U.S. Department of Agriculture.

Known as the Wizard of Tuskegee, Carver received many honors, including election to a fellowship in the Royal Arts Society of London (1917), the NAACP Spingarn Medal for research in agricultural chemistry (1923), the Theodore Roosevelt Medal (1939), and an honorary Doctorate of Science from the University of Rochester (1941). In his later years, he used his life savings of $33,000 to establish the George Washington Carver Foundation for Agricultural Research. Recognized as one of America's outstanding scientists, Carver died in Tuskegee on January 5, 1943.

Charles R. Drew

Benjamin Duggar

Drew, Charles R. A black medical researcher and surgeon, Charles Drew in 1939 developed an effective method of storing and preserving large quantities of blood plasma in what became known as blood banks. Drew discovered that when plasma, the fluid substance of the blood, is separated from the red bloodcells, it could be used to replace lost blood. Drew also discovered that plasma could be frozen or dried into a powder and stored for long periods of time. The discovery made it possible for the first time to have blood fluids stored and available for use in medical emergencies.

Born in 1904 in Washington, D.C., Drew studied medicine at McGill University in Canada and specialized in blood research. After graduating, he continued his research at the Columbia Medical Center in New York, where he made his blood plasma discovery. Early in World War II, Drew formed and directed the British Blood Bank which collected blood in New York, converted it into plasma, and shipped it overseas. Appointed director of the American Red Cross blood bank project in 1941, Drew later resigned when the Red Cross agreed to army and navy insistence that blood from black donors be refused. He publicly stated that there was no scientific difference between blood from persons of different races. While medical director of Freedman's Hospital in Washington, D.C., Drew became recognized as an authority in surgical research. Beginning in 1945, he established recruiting programs for blacks to enter the medical profession. Drew died in an automobile accident in 1950.

Duggar, Benjamin Minge. Discovering aureomycin, the first "broad spectrum" antibiotic drug, in 1944, plant physiologist Benjamin Duggar, at seventy-six years of age, achieved a major breakthrough in man's fight against infectious disease. Duggar developed the drug after examining thousands of soil samples for their ability to kill disease-causing bacteria. Attacking a wide range of bacteria, he developed aureomycin, an effective drug for reducing high fevers and keeping secondary infections from spreading throughout the body.

Born in Alabama in 1872, Duggar became interested at an early age in experimental agriculture and often accompanied the town druggist walking through the woods in a hunt for soils and plant life to use as crude drugs. After graduating from Alabama Polytechnic Institute in 1892, Duggar enrolled at Harvard and received his master's degree in 1895. In 1897 he became an instructor of botany at Cornell, earning his Ph.D. in plant cytology (cell study) in 1898. He helped reorganize the mushroom-growing industry in 1901 by making effective use of scientific growing methods. Duggar also developed a system for detecting deterioration in potato-breeding stocks and studied the little-known tobacco virus. From 1927 to 1943 he taught at the University of Wisconsin. The following year Duggar joined a chemical firm and began research in fields other than agriculture. Within two years he isolated the soil cultures that led to aureomycin. His discovery opened new areas of research. Duggar died in 1956.

EINSTEIN

Albert Einstein

Einstein, Albert. Considered the most creative scientist since Isaac Newton, Albert Einstein laid the foundation for the modern Nuclear Age. Einstein's three revolutionary papers, published in 1905 when he was only 26 years old, destroyed the structure of physics as it was then known, giving man a completely new understanding of the universe. Born in Germany in 1879, Einstein did poorly in school, spending most of his time teaching himself physics and mathematics. After graduating from Polytechnic Institute in Zurich, Switzerland, he worked in the Swiss patent office.

Einstein's first paper expanded Max Planck's quantum theory to explain the behavior of all energy emissions. Einstein later was awarded the Nobel Prize in 1921 because his explanation of this "photoelectric effect" began the new physics of quantum mechanics.

His second paper, giving a mathematical explanation of "Brownian motion," accurately described the motion of particles suspended in a drop of water. Using Einstein's calculations, other scientists were able to calculate the size of a molecule and for the first time prove the existence of atoms within the molecules.

Einstein's third paper, the "Special Theory of Relativity," provided a totally new view of the universe. He showed that matter and energy are not different and can be interchanged. But, when converted, small amounts of matter are changed into vast amounts of energy. Einstein explained this in his famous equation: $E = MC^2$. He also showed that time and distance, absolute values on earth, are relative in space and will vary with the motion of the observer; only the speed of light, at 186,000 miles per second, is constant and unchanging throughout the universe. In 1915 Einstein published his "General Theory of Relativity," replacing Newton's theories.

Lecturing in California when Germany came under Nazi rule, Einstein decided to immigrate to the U.S. Moving to the Institute for Advanced Study at Princeton, New Jersey, he attempted to complete work on a "Unified Field Theory," combining the theories of electromagnetic effects and gravitation. In 1939, Einstein wrote to President Roosevelt, urging him to begin research on an atomic bomb. Six years later, scientists applied Einstein's theories to create the bomb—ushering in the Atomic Age. In 1955 Einstein, still working on his Unified Field Theory, died in Princeton. After his death, atomic element 99 (Einsteinium) was named in his honor.

Joseph Erlanger

Enrico Fermi

Erlanger, Joseph. Doctor, physiologist, and pioneer in research on the human nervous system, Joseph Erlanger, with his associate Herbert Gasser, won the 1944 Nobel Prize in medicine and physiology. The citation read: "For their discoveries regarding the highly differentiated functions of single nerve fibers." Erlanger and Gasser sent electrical charges through nerve fibers, discovering the mechanism by which nerve functions are created. This became the basis for future work in neurophysiology. Born in California in 1874, Erlanger received his medical degree at Johns Hopkins University in 1899 and began his work with Gasser in the early 1900s at Washington University. They researched together in nerve functions until they shared the 1944 Nobel Prize. Erlanger retired in 1948 as chairman of the physiology department of the Medical School of Washington University. He died in St. Louis in 1965.

Fermi, Enrico. The first man to direct a self-sustaining chain reaction of nuclear particles, physicist Enrico Fermi on December 2, 1942 proved that the unrealized power of atomic energy was controllable and possible to use. Fermi's nuclear reactor, located under the football stands at the University of Chicago, shot a stream of neutrons—electromagnetic particles—into the nucleus of uranium 235 atoms, causing them to split apart. The split released large amounts of energy and unleashed additional neutrons which split other uranium atoms in a continuous process. The tremendous power created by nuclear reaction was later harnessed for use in weapons of war, to produce electricity, and to propel ships.

Born in 1901 in Italy, Fermi received his Ph.D. from the University of Pisa in 1922. Beginning his study of the neutron following its discovery in 1932, he developed a system to slow its speed and use the neutrons to bombard chemical elements. In 1934 he bombarded uranium with his slow neutrons, but the results were confusing. An Italian citizen, Fermi strongly opposed the fascist government and its racial laws against Jews, which were a threat to his Jewish wife. In 1938 he traveled with his family to Sweden to receive the Nobel Prize for physics and then came to America. Later, he learned that he had not created a higher element as he believed, but had split the uranium atom. When the U.S. organized the Manhattan Project in 1942, Fermi directed the development of the first controlled nuclear chain reactor. He died in 1954.

James Franck

Casimir Funk

Franck, James. A Nobel Prize-winning physicist (1925) for his bombarding of atoms to test their energy, James Franck during World War II applied his early experiments to the development of the atomic bomb. For his study of the way plants absorb light to make food, he was given the Rumford Medal of the American Academy of Arts and Sciences in 1955. Born in 1882 in Germany, Franck received his Ph.D. at the University of Berlin in 1906. After 13 years as a professor at the University of Gottingen, he strongly protested Nazi government policies and immigrated to the U.S. Appointed a professor at the University of Chicago in 1938, he became a participant in the early experiments to control the chain reaction caused by the fission of atomic energy. Opposed to the atomic bomb and its deadly effects, he proposed a demonstration before representatives of other countries. Franck died in 1964.

Funk, Casimir. Searching for a cure in the early 1900s for the Far East nutritional disease of beriberi, biochemist Casimir Funk discovered that specific foods produce chemical effects in the body that help resist many diseases. He called these disease fighting elements vitamins. Born in 1884 in Poland, Funk as a boy wanted to be a biologist. His father, a doctor, persuaded him to study biochemistry. After receiving his Ph.D. at the University of Berne in Switzerland in 1904, he worked at research institutes in Paris and Berlin. In 1910 Funk moved to the Lister Institute of Preventative Medicine in London, where he began researching the idea that a diet limited to polished rice causes beriberi.

Using pigeons for his experiments, Funk found he could cure a type of beriberi by feeding the birds rice husk, the part removed when rice is polished. He discovered that one ton of rice husks contains only one ounce of the needed antiberiberi food. When he announced his findings in 1912, he theorized that a number of diseases were caused by a lack of what he termed "vitamines," a word coined from "vita" (Latin for "life") and "amine," a chemical compound that he believed was found in some foods. Funk labeled his finding Vitamin B_1. In 1913 he wrote the book *Die Vitamine*, explaining the physiological importance of vitamins as food elements. Funk traveled to the U.S. in 1915 to begin his work on cancer research. He returned to Poland in 1923 to become chief of the State Institute of Hygiene. Funk settled permanently in the U.S. in 1939 and conducted cancer research. Funk died in 1967.

George Gamow

Ross Granville Harrison

Gamow, George. To discover the way stars are formed and die and the way atoms in outer space come together to form stars, astronomer George Gamow, starting in the 1930s, studied the nature of the universe. Unlike other scientists, Gamow was able to explain his theories in terms that could be understood by the non-astronomer. He wrote many books to popularize his scientific theories and illustrated some with his own amusing drawings. Scientists in the 1930s already understood that stars operate on atomic fuels, but Gamow proved that stars heat up, rather than cool down, as hydrogen, their basic atomic fuel, is burned away. To support the theory that the universe began with an explosion in the distant past, Gamow believed that many of the atoms now existing could have been formed when the explosion occurred.

Gamow worked in several different fields of science, including nuclear physics, biology, and astronomy. His studies in biochemistry in 1954 advanced a theory explaining how living cells could pass their characteristics from one generation to another. His theory was later proven to be basically correct. Born in Russia in 1904, George Gamow was the grandson of a general in the Russian army. A small telescope given him on his thirteenth birthday by his father aroused Gamow's interest in science. He obtained his Ph.D. at the University of Leningrad in 1928, furthered his studies in other countries, and finally settled in 1934 in the United States. He wrote and taught at several universities. Gamow died in 1968.

Harrison, Ross Granville. The biologist who first grew living tissue cultures outside the body, Ross Harrison in the early 1900s discovered secrets of how animals and human beings develop as embryos before birth. Using unborn amphibians in laboratory analysis, he experimented with tissues in a life-giving substance called a culture medium and formulated sets of rules for growth patterns of body parts in various embryos. In 1907, Harrison demonstrated an important experiment on the outgrowth of embryo nerve fibers in a culture medium. This experiment led to an understanding of the human nervous system.

Born in 1870 in Pennsylvania, Harrison earned a Ph.D. at Johns Hopkins University in 1894. He taught at Bryn Mawr College for a year and left to attend the University of Bonn in Germany, where he earned an M.D. in 1899. Harrison taught anatomy at Johns Hopkins until 1907, when he was appointed chairman of the Zoology Department at Yale, a post he held until his retirement in 1938. Harrison then became chairman of the National Research Council until 1946 and provided essential services to the U.S. during World War II. Harrison was an early editor of the *Journal of Morphology* and for 42 years was also managing editor of the *Journal of Experimental Zoology*. Some of his important research included transplantation of amphibian larvae, adaptation of the hanging-drop culture method to the study of embryonic tissues, and fin development in fishes. Harrison also invented devices for tissue grafting. He died in 1959.

Philip S. Hench **Harry Hammond Hess** **Victor Francis Hess**

Hench, Philip S. For his work in the discovery and application of cortisone, a synthetic medicine used in the treatment of arthritis, Philip Hench in 1950 shared the Nobel Prize for physiology and medicine. Born in 1896 in Pittsburgh, Hench received his medical degree at the University of Pittsburgh in 1920. He was appointed to the staff of the Mayo Foundation in 1921 and in 1926 was selected as director of the rheumatic diseases department. Hench noticed that the swelling caused by arthritis was eased in pregnant women and in patients suffering from jaundice. He found that specific chemicals in the body called steroids lessened the pain in arthritic sufferers. Working with Edward Kendall, he determined in 1948 the methods to manufacture a synthetic medicine (cortisone) that acted like steroids. The team also found cortisone was helpful in treating burns and skin conditions. Hench died in 1965.

Hess, Harry Hammond. Searching the world's oceans during the 1940s, geologist Harry Hess found their deepest points and lofty underwater mountains. A submarine base commander and admiral during World War II, Hess was a specialist in the geology of the ocean floor. Born in 1906 in New York City, he received his Ph.D. at Princeton University and became a faculty member in 1934. During 1945, his soundings made from submarines found the deepest ocean floor near the Philippines, seven miles below the surface. The next year, he discovered hundreds of sea mountains whose flat tops tower above the ocean floor. Naming them "guyots," Hess theorized they had been islands before they sank. A professor and head of Princeton's Department of Geology, he was also an adviser to the U.S. space program. Just before the first moon landing, which he had helped plan, Hess died in 1969.

Hess, Victor Francis. The first man to determine that radiation comes from outer space, Victor Hess, beginning in 1911, made ten balloon ascents to find cosmic rays. Born in 1883 in Austria, Hess received a Ph.D. from the University of Graz in 1920. After years of research and teaching at the Vienna Academy of Sciences, in 1938 Hess and his wife fled from Nazi Germany to the United States, where he joined the faculty at Fordham University. In 1944 he became an American citizen and after World War II began studying the measurement of radioactive fallout from nuclear bombs. Hess's earlier balloon experiments proved that radiation comes from outer space and not, as previously thought, from the soil. He also found that the radiation measured eight times greater than that on the ground. Hess, who shared the 1936 Nobel Prize in physics with Carl Anderson, died in 1964.

William A. Hinton

Edwin Powell Hubble

Hinton, William A. A medical scientist who was an international authority on venereal diseases, William Hinton in 1925 developed a reliable medical test to detect the presence of syphilis in the body. He wrote a textbook on the study of syphilis and, with Dr. J. A. V. Davies, he discovered a second test for the disease. Born in 1883 in Chicago, Hinton received his medical degree from Harvard University in 1912. After three years as a voluntary laboratory assistant at Massachusetts General Hospital, he was appointed director of the Boston Dispensary laboratory, a post he held for 36 years. In 1921 Hinton began teaching immunology and bacteriology at Harvard University Medical School and in 1949 became the first black granted a Harvard professorship at the medical school. He was also a consultant to the U.S. Public Health Service. Hinton died in Massachusetts in 1959.

Hubble, Edwin Powell. Discoverer of facts about galaxies of stars in outer space, astronomer Edwin Hubble completed research early in the 1900s which established the vast size of the known universe beyond our solar system. Born in 1889 in Missouri, Hubble received a degree in law as a Rhodes scholar at Oxford University. After returning to the U.S., he accepted a position at Yerkes Observatory. He served in France during World War I, and in 1920 Hubble joined the staff of Mount Wilson Observatory in California, where he studied individual stars within the Andromeda nebula.

In 1923 Hubble found some of the stars in Andromeda to be Cepheid variables, whose light patterns determine the star's distance from earth. The starlight from the Cepheids proved that Andromeda lay far beyond the earth's galaxy. Other nebulae were discovered to be farther away and in various shapes and forms. Hubble classified the galaxies according to the number found in an area and where they were distributed in the sky. His theories suggested the way stars were formed and their ages. In 1929 Hubble suggested that galaxies in space were moving away from the earth at speeds directly proportional to their distance from the earth. This factor was named Hubble's Constant, and he used the formula to postulate the outer limits of the universe. From this formula, Hubble estimated that the galaxies were formed about two billion years ago. Hubble's estimates were later proved in error, but his work led to an understanding of the expansion of the universe. He died in 1953.

Ernest Everett Just   **Edward C. Kendall**   **Karl Landsteiner**

Just, Ernest Everett. An international authority in the field of cytology—the study of living cells—black scientist Ernest Just conducted experiments which explained the behavior of cancer cells in the human body. Born in South Carolina in 1883, Just attended Dartmouth on a scholarship and graduated with honors. He earned his Ph.D. at the University of Chicago in 1916. Just taught at Howard University and conducted summer research experiments at the Marine Biological Laboratory at Woods Hole, Massachusetts. This work led him to the investigation of cancer cells. After publishing many papers and two books on his discoveries of cell behavior, Just served as vice-president of the American Society of Zoologists. In 1915 Just was awarded the first Spingarn Medal by the NAACP. During the 1930s, Just also conducted research in Europe. He died in 1941.

Kendall, Edward C. For his work in developing the drug that became known as cortisone and for its general application in the treatment of rheumatoid arthritis, biochemist Edward Kendall was awarded the 1950 Nobel Prize in medicine and shared it with associates. Kendall, born in Connecticut in 1886, was educated at Columbia University, receiving his Ph.D. in chemistry in 1910. He joined the Mayo Clinic in 1914 as chief of the biochemistry division and began research into the functions of the thyroid gland. Soon, Kendall discovered a method of separating a chemical from the gland for use in treating defects in human growth. Following his thyroid research, Kendall and his associates conducted studies of the adrenal gland, separating six different hormones. Further experiments proved that one hormone, cortisone, is beneficial in treating rheumatoid arthritis. Kendall died in 1972.

Landsteiner, Karl. For discovering the four basic human blood groups, Karl Landsteiner won the 1930 Nobel Prize for medicine and made possible lifesaving transfusions through the matching of blood for compatibility. Until Landsteiner's discovery, many countries banned transfusions. Landsteiner's four blood groups, A, B, AB, and O, were established in 1902. By 1927 he added groups M, N, and MN. Born in 1868 in Austria, Landsteiner received his medical degree at the University of Vienna. He became a professor of pathology in 1908 and was the first to isolate the polio virus. Invited to the U.S. in 1922, he continued his research at the Rockefeller Institute. After retiring in 1939, Landsteiner identified a blood factor which, when present in certain combinations, could prove dangerous to newborn infants. He named the factor "RH" after experiments on rhesus monkeys. He died in 1943.

Irving Langmuir

Ernest Orlando Lawrence

Langmuir, Irving. Experimenting with gas-filled electric light bulbs, Irving Langmuir developed an improved fixture that extended the light-time of the bulb and for discoveries in the field of surface chemistry was awarded a Nobel Prize in 1932. Langmuir's creative approach to the electric bulb included the study of the effects of gases on hot metal surfaces and the reaction of molecules to the surface. Langmuir was born in 1881 in New York. He developed an early interest in science and carried on independent studies in a home laboratory. After graduating from Columbia in 1903, he was awarded his Ph.D. in chemistry at the University of Göttingen in Germany.

Returning to the United States, Langmuir taught chemistry at the Stevens Institute of Technology, and in 1909 he joined the research staff of a large electric company in New York where he remained until his retirement in 1950. Following his discovery that increased the working time of light bulbs, Langmuir devised an atomic hydrogen blowtorch in 1925 that produced an extremely high temperature jet. In 1930, Langmuir developed a mercury condensation vacuum pump which led to methods of producing high-vacuum tubes for use in electronic products. He also studied how atoms form bonds with each other and helped establish a new theory of electronic bonding. During World War II, Langmuir searched for a method to prevent dangerous ice from forming on aircraft in flight. The research led to the first man-made "rainmaking" process. He died in 1957.

Lawrence, Ernest Orlando. The 1939 Nobel Prize in physics was awarded to Ernest O. Lawrence for his invention of the cyclotron, the first large-scale atomic particle accelerator. Lawrence's 80-ton, drum-shaped device, built in 1933, accelerated charged protons by magnetic pushes until they increased in speed and energy to penetrate the nucleus of an atom. Lawrence's cyclotron changed stable forms of many elements into radioactive isotopes. During World War II, the cyclotron was put to use to separate the initial samples of highly fissionable uranium 235 from natural uranium. The cyclotron produced the necessary fuel to fire the first atomic explosion.

Lawrence was born in 1901 in South Dakota and attended St. Olaf College before graduating from the University of South Dakota in 1922. He attended Yale as a National Research fellow and received his Ph.D. in 1925. In 1927 he joined the faculty of the University of California and in 1936 became director of the radiation laboratory at the school. After experiments with his first cyclotron, Lawrence built larger cyclotrons in 1938 and 1942 to create more powerful magnetic fields. During the U.S. atomic bomb crash-program starting in 1941, Lawrence directed a staff of more than 5,000 scientists searching for an efficient process to produce atomic fuel. After the war, Lawrence conducted research on artificial radioactive elements and added to the understanding of nuclear physics. In 1957 he received the Fermi Prize from the Atomic Energy Commission. Lawrence died in 1958.

Gilbert Newton Lewis   **Elmer V. McCollum**   **Maria Goeppert Mayer**

Lewis, Gilbert Newton. By suggesting that a bond between two chemical elements could be formed through the sharing of electrons, chemist Gilbert Lewis established the foundation of the modern theory of valence in 1916. Valence—the measure of the ability of an atom to combine with other like or different atoms—was proven when Lewis found one pair of electrons sharing each bond in various organic compounds. Stable electronic shapes of molecular structures in chemical compounds could be explained by Lewis's discovery. Born in Massachusetts in 1875, Lewis received his Ph.D degree from Harvard in 1899. He was appointed dean of the College of Chemistry at the University of California in 1912. In 1923 he wrote *Thermodynamics and the Free Energy of Chemical Substances*. In 1933 Lewis isolated deuterium, hydrogen's heavy isotope, used in the hydrogen bomb. He died in 1946.

McCollum, Elmer V. Experimenting with white rats that were fed different combinations of foods, biochemist Elmer McCollum learned in 1913 that factors essential to life are present in some fats and discovered the need for vitamins in the human diet. McCollum's discoveries were named vitamin A and vitamin B, and they became the first of many vitamins later isolated. McCollum contributed to the discovery of both vitamin D in 1922 and vitamin E a few years later. Born in Kansas, McCollum graduated from the University of Kansas in 1903, received his Ph.D. at Yale in 1906, and joined the University of Wisconsin faculty in 1907. He became professor of biochemistry at Johns Hopkins University in 1917 and remained there until his retirement in 1946. McCollum determined that small quantities of minerals, including calcium, are necessary to sustain life. He died in 1967.

Mayer, Maria Goeppert. Sharing the 1963 Nobel Prize in physics for her research on the atomic nucleus, Maria Mayer became the first U.S. woman and the first woman since Madame Curie to win the high award. Born in Germany in 1906, Maria Goeppert received her Ph.D. in 1930 from the University of Göttingen. After marrying and immigrating to America, she was appointed professor of physics at the University of Chicago in 1946. In 1948 Dr. Mayer advanced the theory that the nucleus of the atom—its core—consists of spinning protons and neutrons arranged in shells, an arrangement that electrons outside the nucleus were already known to possess. The so-called "magic numbers" of her shells explained why some nuclei are more stable than others. In 1960 Dr. Mayer was named to the faculty of the University of California at San Diego. She died in 1972.

Robert A. Millikan

Millikan, Robert A. For his achievement in measuring the size and electrical charge of a single electron and his experimental work in confirming Einstein's equation on the photo-electric effect—changes in electrons caused by visible light—physicist Robert Millikan received the Nobel Prize in physics in 1923. Millikan found that all electrons have the same small charge. To reach his conclusion, he suspended a tiny drop of oil in a chamber by balancing an upward electromagnetic pull with the downward pull of gravity. After using x-rays to charge the droplet with electricity, he measured the size of the charge by finding the amount and direction it moved. By identifying individual units in an electrical charge, this experiment was final proof that electricity is made up of separate particles.

Millikan was born in Illinois in 1868 and graduated from Oberlin College in 1891. While studying for his master's degree at Oberlin, he taught several physics classes. In 1895 he obtained a Ph.D. degree in physics from Columbia University. He continued his studies in Germany in 1895-96, then returned to the U.S to teach at the University of Chicago, where he worked with another American physicist, Albert Michelson, and began his experiments on elec-trical charges and the photoelectric effect. Appointed a full professor in 1910, he received the Comstock Prize of the National Academy of Sciences in 1913 for his work in setting apart and measuring the electron.

During World War I, Millikan was chief of the science and research division of the Army Signal Corps. After the war he became director of the Norman Bridge Laboratory of the California Institute of Technology (Caltech), where he remained until retiring in 1946. While there, Millikan started studies on radiation (waves or particles) coming from outer space, and in 1925 he named the radiation cosmic rays. During World War II, he helped develop rocket-propulsion systems.

Millikan wrote many scientific books, including *Electricity, Sound and Light* (1908), *The Electron* (1917), and *Cosmic Rays* (1939). He received many honors and awards, including the Hughes Medal from the Royal Society of Great Britain (1923), Matteucci Medal from the Societa Italiana della Scienza (1925), and gold medals from the Society of Arts and Sciences and the American Society of Mechanical Engineering. He was also president of the American Association for the Advancement of Science. Millikan died in 1953.

George R. Minot

Hermann J. Muller

Minot, George R. Suspecting that the lack of vitamins caused pernicious anemia, physician George Minot discovered in 1926 that liver included in a patient's diet was an effective treatment for the disease. Minot believed that the reduction of red corpuscles in the blood, resulting in pernicious anemia, was caused by the absence of specific vitamins and in 1924 began feeding liver to his anemic patients. He worked with Dr. William Murphy, and by 1926 they were able to report dramatic improvements in the red blood corpuscle counts of pernicious anemia patients. For their discovery, Minot and Murphy, together with G. H. Whipple, who had made earlier studies of the disease, were awarded the 1934 Nobel Prize in medicine. Born in 1885, Minot received his medical degree from Harvard University in 1912. In 1928 he was named a professor at Harvard. Minot died in 1950.

Muller, Hermann J. By discovering in 1926 that x-rays can cause artificial mutations (changes) in fruit flies that can be passed along to future generations, biologist Hermann Muller influenced the study of heredity—the spreading of characteristics from parents to offspring. He later found that certain conditions could cause harmful changes in humans, which could be reproduced in their children. For his work, Muller was awarded the 1946 Nobel Prize in medicine and physiology.

Muller was born in 1890 in New York and received his master's degree in 1911 and Ph.D. in 1916 from Columbia University. There he worked with scientist Thomas Hunt Morgan and helped discover the existence of genes—carriers of heredity. He studied and worked in Europe from 1932 to 1940, dividing his time between Germany, Russia, and Scotland. During this period he proposed that the human race could be improved through eugenics—the matching of good characteristics in parents that could be passed along to children. In 1940 he joined the faculty of Amherst College, and in 1945 he was appointed professor of zoology at Indiana University. After World War II Muller joined other scientists, including Albert Einstein, in opposing atomic bombs. He warned that harmful changes could occur in all living creatures, including humans, as a result of fallout in the air after an atomic explosion. Muller was coauthor of *Genetics, Medicine and Man* and wrote *Out of the Night, A Biologist's View of the Future* and *Studies in Genetics*. He died in 1967.

J. Robert Oppenheimer

Oppenheimer, J. Robert. Director of the U.S. Los Alamos Scientific Laboratory (1943–1945), physicist J. Robert Oppenheimer led in the development of the first atomic bomb, which forced the Japanese surrender ending World War II. Comparing several possible designs for assembling the bomb, Oppenheimer chose the method that led to its production in less than three years. Believing that the bomb program should be concentrated in one place, Oppenheimer selected a remote area in New Mexico where he assembled 4,500 scientists. The first atomic bomb was tested July 16, 1945. Later that year, one was exploded over Hiroshima, Japan. For his work on the bomb, Oppenheimer was awarded the Presidential Citation and Medal of Merit. He was appointed chairman of the General Advisory Committee of the Atomic Energy Commission (AEC), serving from 1946 to 1952. Oppenheimer pressed for strong United Nations control of all nuclear weapons produced by the United States and other countries.

Oppenheimer was born in New York in 1904 and graduated from Harvard University in 1926. He studied atomic research under Lord Rutherford at Cambridge and obtained his Ph.D. in 1927 at Göttingen University, studying under Max Born. In 1929 he joined the faculty of California Institute of Technology and investigated relativistic high-energy phenomena, helped discover the positron, and explained cosmic ray showers. Oppenheimer's studies in 1939 of the amount of uranium needed to set off an atomic explosion led to his assignment in 1942 to build the bomb. In 1947 he became the director of the Institute for Advanced Studies at Princeton University, where he continued his research in physics until his retirement in 1966.

Oppenheimer maintained a broad interest in the arts, classics, poetry, and plays. He could read in eight languages. His wide cultural interests and social concern led him to support many idealistic causes. During the late 1930s, he became involved in certain movements of the Communist party that were active in the Spanish civil war. Although he proved he was never a member of the party, the Atomic Energy Commission, yielding to testimony made against him during the 1950s, labeled Oppenheimer "a loyal citizen but not a good security risk." President Eisenhower removed his security clearance, which cut him off from government research. In 1963 the Atomic Energy Commission awarded Oppenheimer its highest honor, the Fermi Award, attempting to make amends for their earlier action against him. Oppenheimer died in 1967.

Wolfgang Pauli

Francis P. Rous

Pauli, Wolfgang. For his work in advancing the understanding of atomic structure through his discovery of the exclusion principle, physicist Wolfgang Pauli was awarded the 1945 Nobel Prize in physics. Before Pauli, quantum theory had stipulated that electrons orbiting around the atomic nucleus can exist only in certain special energy states or levels. Pauli's exclusion principle, announced in 1925, added that it would be impossible for more than one electron to lie in any one of these states—once an energy level is filled, all other electrons are excluded. Pauli's exclusion principle explained why electrons form concentric shells around the atom's nucleus, each holding only a limited number of electrons. It also accounted for the highly reactive nature of some elements—such as chlorine—that have in the outermost shell only one electron, which is easily lost to any other element needing it. Atomic weights and chemical properties could be explained by the different numbers of shells.

Pauli was born in 1900 in Austria and received his Ph.D. from the University of Munich. In 1923 he joined the faculty of the University of Hamburg and in 1928 moved to the Zürich Institute of Technology. As early as 1931 he suggested the existence of a new particle, with neither charge nor mass, required to maintain the law of the conservation of energy. Although Enrico Fermi in 1932 named it the "neutrino," Pauli had to wait until 1956 for its existence to be confirmed. Pauli joined the Institute for Advanced Study at Princeton in 1940. He died in Switzerland in 1958.

Rous, Francis P. Studying a tumor on a chicken brought in by a farmer, medical researcher Francis Rous discovered in 1911 the first virus known to cause cancer. Rous ground up the tumor, filtered away the cells, and injected the fine remains into other chickens. When they developed tumors, Rous believed that the infected substance, since it had passed through the filter, was a tiny virus. But scientists doubted his cancer experiments, and it was more than 50 years before Rous's contributions were recognized by being awarded a share of the 1966 Nobel Prize for medicine. Born in Maryland in 1879, Rous received his M.D. in 1905 from Johns Hopkins. In 1909 he was appointed a medical researcher at the Rockefeller Institute. During World War I, Rous discovered a method of preserving blood, which led to the first blood banks. Continuing his medical study on the liver and gall bladder until age 90, Rous died in 1970.

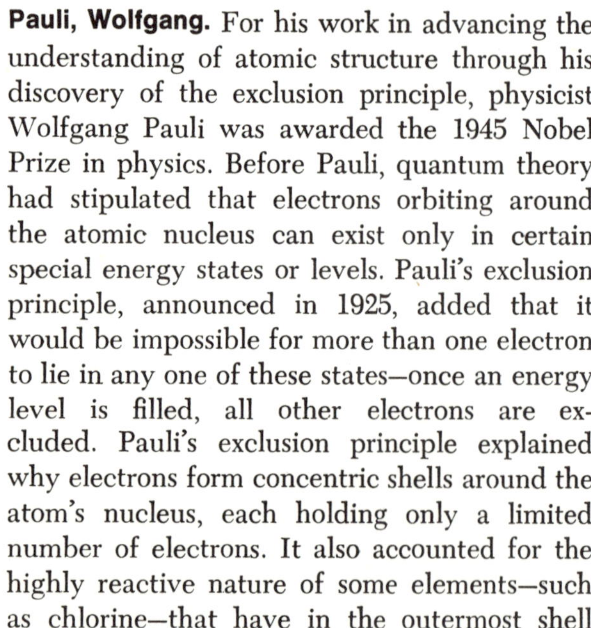

Manfred Sakel

Rudolf Schoenheimer

Sakel, Manfred. Discovering a treatment for schizophrenia (split personality), psychiatrist Manfred Sakel made a substantial medical advance toward its treatment by administering insulin shock therapy starting in 1927. Born in Austria in 1900, Sakel studied for four years at Brno in Czechoslovakia. In 1925 he received his medical degree from the University of Vienna and in 1927 was appointed director of Lichterfelde Hospital in Berlin, where he began treating morphine addicts with insulin to reduce their desire for the drug. He accidentally administered an overdose of insulin, and the patient was shocked into unconsciousness. When Sakel revived him, the patient's mind, previously confused, was now shown to be clear. Sakel next decided to try the treatment on a schizophrenic patient—after first preparing to flee from Berlin should it fail. The treatment proved successful, and Sakel devoted his career to teaching and researching insulin shock treatment.

Sakel immigrated to the U.S. in 1936 and was quickly invited to explain his treatment to New York doctors. He refused numerous offers to join universities, preferring instead to become associated with the New York Department of Mental Health. A study of patients at the Brooklyn State Hospital treated with insulin shocks, pioneered by Sakel, revealed that 55 percent recovered sufficiently to live useful lives. In 1945 Sakel helped establish the Manfred Sakel Foundation to provide training and experience for medical men in the Sakel treatment. Sakel died in 1957. His early death was attributed in part to the strain of his practice.

Schoenheimer, Rudolf. A scientist who fled to America when Hitler came to power in Germany, biochemist Rudolf Schoenheimer perfected the use of radioactive tracers—tiny atomic particles—whose movements inside a plant or animal could be followed with scientific detection instruments. Born in 1898 in Berlin, Schoenheimer received a Ph.D. at the University of Berlin. After fleeing Germany, he immigrated to America in 1933 and joined the faculty of Columbia University's College of Physicians and Surgeons. He studied the earlier use of lead isotope atoms by biochemists to observe internal movements in plants and animals. Learning that lead isotopes were poisonous when placed in contact with living tissues, Schoenheimer sought a nonpoisonous isotope.

In 1935 an isotope of hydrogen, called deuterium, became available to researchers. Deuterium is found naturally in living tissues, and Schoenheimer discovered it could be used to trace the absorption of fat molecules in an animal. He added deuterium to the food of laboratory animals and noted how animals consume and store fat in their bodies. His studies showed that stored fat did not constantly remain in the body and was used when a food was required. He also found that as stored fat was used, fresh, ingested fat replaced the stored fat. Schoenheimer was able to trace almost half of the new deuterized fat in the experimental animals. He later discovered how the body absorbs amino acids (protein molecules), the organic compounds necessary for human life and growth. Schoenheimer took his life in 1941.

Harlow Shapley

Vesto Slipher

Shapley, Harlow. A young astronomer who had just graduated from college, Harlow Shapley startled the scientific world in 1917 with evidence that the sun and earth do not lie in the center of the Milky Way galaxy, but on its outer rim. Shapley's discovery was compared to that of Copernicus, who found in the 16th century that the earth is not the center of the universe. Shapley's observations opened the way for the study of the size and shape of the Milky Way galaxy and the vast ocean of stars and planets in which the earth's solar system is located. He demonstrated that the galaxy is much larger than previously had been believed and that many of the clusters of stars called nebulae actually are galaxies.

Born in Missouri in 1885, Shapley graduated from the University of Missouri in 1910, earned a Ph.D. from Princeton in 1913, and joined the staff of the Mount Wilson Observatory in California. Between 1915 and 1920, Shapley photographed and studied the densely packed groups of stars called globular clusters and measured their distances. He noted that they were distributed in a sphere about a center in the constellation Sagittarius. He concluded that the sun was 50,000 light-years from the constellation center, a figure later reduced to 30,000 light-years. In 1921 Shapley was appointed director of the Harvard Observatory, where he served until 1952. Author of many popular and scientific works on astronomy, Shapley was president of the American Academy of Arts and Sciences (1939-1944). He died in Boulder, Colorado in 1972.

Slipher, Vesto M. By demonstrating that most of the large clusters of stars known as nebulae are moving away from the earth, astronomer Vesto Slipher in 1912 laid the foundation for the theory of the "expanding universe." Slipher's theory suggests that the stars are moving farther and farther apart and is based on his discovery of the phenomenon he named the "red shift"—a change in the structure of light coming from a nebula, showing whether the nebula was moving toward or away from Earth. Slipher was able to develop this and other significant discoveries with the help of the spectroscope, an instrument used in analyzing the structure of light. He also organized and directed research which led to the discovery of the planet Pluto in 1930 and became the first astronomer to obtain clear photographs of the surface of Mars. Slipher is also credited as the first to analyze the atmospheres of the planets Jupiter, Saturn, and Neptune.

Slipher was born on a farm in Indiana in 1875 and attended Indiana University, receiving a Ph.D. in 1909. He was named assistant director of Lowell Observatory in Flagstaff, Arizona in 1915, and in 1916 he was promoted to acting director of the observatory, a position he held until his retirement in 1952. In his studies, he found more accurate methods of measuring the rotations of the planets. Slipher was awarded many honors in his life, among them a tribute from another outstanding astronomer who wrote: "It is difficult to name an astronomer who has made a larger number of important discoveries." Slipher died in 1969.

Wendell M. Stanley

James B. Sumner

Stanley, Wendell M. A chemist fascinated by the puzzle of the tiny disease-causing organisms called viruses, Wendell Stanley succeeded in 1935 in growing a virus and proved that it consisted of protein. Stanley's breakthrough opened a large field of research that led to far-reaching advances in medicine and basic science, and in 1946 he shared the Nobel Prize for chemistry. Born in Indiana in 1904, Stanley played football at Earlham College and intended to become a football coach, but he became so interested in chemistry that he decided to do graduate work. He obtained a Ph.D. at the University of Illinois in 1929, did further graduate work in Germany, and joined the Rockefeller Institute in 1931.

Stanley was aware that other scientists isolated substances called enzymes and found them to be protein, and he undertook to do the same thing with the equally puzzling viruses, growing one on a tobacco plant. The fine, needle-like crystals he obtained from his tobacco experiment amazed the scientific world, since it was believed impossible for living matter, such as a virus, to exist in crystal form. A controversy developed over whether his crystals were actually living matter. Further experimentation showed that many viruses could be crystallized and that all consisted partly of protein and were living. During World War II, Stanley worked on an influenza vaccine later adopted by the U.S. military. In 1948 he established a research laboratory at the University of California and served as its director until 1969. Stanley died in 1971.

Sumner, James B. Despite a boyhood hunting accident that cost him an arm, James Sumner became a research chemist and in 1926 made a discovery about the nature of enzymes—the basic substances that aid in digestion—that won him a Nobel Prize. Because his discovery directly contradicted the research of another Nobel Prize winner, Sumner found himself involved in a fierce dispute, and it took many years for other researchers to prove conclusively that he was right. For that reason Sumner did not receive his Nobel Prize until 1946. Born in Massachusetts in 1887, Sumner, who was left-handed, lost his left arm in 1904. His teachers thought the handicap would ruin his career as a chemist; he disregarded their thinking, graduated from Harvard in 1910, obtained a Ph.D. in 1914, and became an assistant professor at Cornell Medical School, where he began a series of experiments on enzymes.

Some scientists thought enzymes were made of protein, but others disagreed, and a German chemist, Dr. Richard Willstätter, thought he had proved they were not. In 1926 Sumner refrigerated enzymes he had extracted from jack beans and found that he had produced crystals which he was able to identify as protein. Sumner's report aroused opposition among many scientists but also encouraged other U.S. researchers to follow his lead, while he himself went abroad to work with two Swedish scientists. Sumner's work also led to significant research in the related field of viruses and to the development of new vaccines against virus diseases such as influenza and polio. He died in 1955.

Selman Waksman   **Norbert Wiener**   **Robert Williams**

Waksman, Selman. Testing 10,000 chemicals produced by microbes to determine which were capable of stopping the growth of disease-causing bacteria, biochemist Selman Waksman discovered streptomycin in the 1940s—the first effective antibiotic medicine for treating tuberculosis. For his discovery he was awarded the 1952 Nobel Prize in medicine. Waksman originated the term antibiotic ("against life") for the chemicals, obtained from soil microorganisms, capable of killing bacteria. Born in Russia in 1888, Waksman immigrated to the U.S. in 1910 and received a Ph.D. from the University of California in 1918. He joined the faculty of Rutgers University, where he taught until 1958. His research also resulted in the discoveries of Aureomycin, Terramycin, and Neomycin. Waksman wrote two significant books, *My Life with the Microbes* and *The Conquest of Tuberculosis*. He died in 1973.

Wiener, Norbert. Called the Father of Automation, mathematician Norbert Wiener developed the science of automated machine control of information and published his popular book, *Cybernetics*, in 1949. Wiener believed that a similarity existed between highly involved machines, such as automatic computers, and the operation of the human brain and nervous system. He named the new science "cybernetics" from the Greek word for steersman. Wiener was born in 1894 in Missouri and received his Ph.D. from Harvard in 1913 at the age of nineteen. After further study in Europe, he joined the faculty of the Massachusetts Institute of Technology in 1919 and remained at the school for 41 years. During World War II, Wiener helped develop machines that provided automatic information processing of radar and missile guidance systems. He warned man against losing control of his complex machines. Wiener died in 1964.

Williams, Robert. After 20 years of study, chemist Robert Williams isolated vitamin B_1 (later called thiamin) from the husks of natural brown rice in 1933, but it took him until 1936 before he learned its chemical structure so it could be duplicated in a laboratory. He started a worldwide program in the 1940s to add vitamin B_1 to white rice, curing the dread disease, beriberi. Williams found vitamin B_1 was usually lacking in Oriental diets consisting mainly of polished white rice. Born in 1886 in India, Williams, the son of a missionary, received a master's degree in 1908 from the University of Chicago. He returned to the Orient and by 1915 found that by adding brown rice bran to the diet, beriberi could be eliminated. After serving in World War I, he continued his research on the vitamin and in 1925 was appointed chemical director of a large telephone company laboratory, where he worked until 1945. Williams died in 1965.

| **Arnold T. Anderson** | **Carl D. Anderson** | **John Bardeen** |

Anderson, Arnold T. A student and colleague of Albert Einstein, Arnold Anderson, an Iroquois Indian, was a member of the group of scientists who secretly developed atomic energy for the United States during World War II. For his contributions to nuclear research, Anderson won a citation from the U.S. government after the war. Born in 1915 on the Grand River Indian Reservation in Canada, Anderson studied at night to advance his education in science and graduated from MacMaster University. He served in the Canadian army for 5 years, and following World War II, was appointed director of research for a major American chemical company. After holding other administrative positions, Anderson was transferred to the company's public affairs division, where he directed a program to provide equal employment opportunities for minority groups and organized special programs to train unskilled workers.

Anderson, Carl D. For discovering and then confirming the existence of two new particles inside the atom, Carl Anderson shared the Nobel Prize for physics in 1936. Born in 1905 in New York, Anderson received his Ph.D. in 1930 from the California Institute of Technology and became a full professor in 1939. Using a cloud chamber, Anderson photographed cosmic rays from outer space. He observed that when the rays struck earth, two new particles were created which behaved unlike anything observed before. The positron left a new curved track that suggested a positive charged electron. His term negatron for the ordinary negatively charged electron never caught on. Later, he and a co-worker identified meson as a heavy electron, which also broke into several tiny particles within a fraction of a second. Anderson continued teaching at Cal Tech and headed research projects that studied cosmic rays.

Bardeen, John. The first person to win two Nobel Prizes in the same field, physicist John Bardeen in 1956 and 1972 was honored for his discoveries in superconductivity—lack of resistance in chilled metals or alloys to the flow of electricity. Research by Bardeen and two other physicists resulted in their 1948 invention of the transistor—a device that duplicated most operations of the vacuum tube although only one-fifteenth of its size. Born in Wisconsin in 1908, Bardeen received a master's degree in electrical engineering from the University of Wisconsin and a Ph.D. in mathematics and physics from Princeton. In 1945 he became a research physicist for a telephone laboratory, where the transistor was invented. In 1951 he became professor of electrical engineering and physics at the University of Illinois, where he and two coworkers conducted research that won the 1972 Nobel Prize.

George Wells Beadle   **Seymour Benzer**   **Lipman Bers**

Beadle, George Wells. For discovering a link between chemistry and genetics—the science of biological heredity—George Beadle and a co-worker shared the 1958 Nobel Prize for medicine and physiology. Their findings shifted the study of genetics from the physical characteristics to a biochemical base. To learn how chemical reactions within living cells affect the development of natural characteristics, they used x-rays to attack a form of mold. The mold was genetically changed, which showed the nutrient compounds necessary for growth and indicated how genes in the human body supervise chemical changes. Born in Nebraska in 1903, Beadle studied at the University of Nebraska and in 1931 earned a Ph.D. from Cornell. After teaching at Harvard, Stanford, and the California Institute of Technology, he was appointed chancellor of the University of Chicago in 1961 and served until 1968.

Benzer, Seymour. Biologist Seymour Benzer in the 1950s discovered that genes, the microscopic units of heredity, can be broken into hundreds of parts and each part identified by its position. Studying a type of virus that invades bacteria, Benzer found a way to detect at which points the chromosomes (strings of genes) were broken when the virus was mutated (genetically changed), and what took place when the break occurred in the middle of a gene. To establish chromosome mapping, he had to isolate and study thousands of mutated viruses individually. Benzer, born in 1921, received his Ph.D. from Purdue, where he helped develop solid state electronic devices for use in radar. Hoping to apply laws of physics to living things, he spent years studying biology. In 1952, as a member of Purdue's faculty, he began his work with viruses. Benzer was elected to the National Academy of Sciences in 1961.

Bers, Lipman. Ordered out of his native Latvia for antigovernment activities, Lipman Bers fled to Czechoslovakia, and then to the U.S. in 1940, where he followed a distinguished career in mathematics. Born in 1914, Bers worked to solve the relationship between complex function theory and elliptic partial differential equations. He revealed areas shared by the two mathematical fields and opened up new directions of mathematical thought, including pioneer work in the theory of moduli, which defines the absolute numerical value of a complex number. After immigrating to the U.S., Bers took part in a war research and training program for the practical use of mathematics held at Brown University. He taught at Syracuse and Columbia universities and conducted mathematical research at Princeton's Institute for Advanced Study. Bers was elected to the National Academy of Sciences in 1964.

Hans Bethe   **Felix Bloch**   **Konrad E. Bloch**

Bethe, Hans. Winner of the 1967 Nobel Prize for physics, Hans Bethe made important advances in the study of nuclear science. In 1938 he discovered the energy sources of stars and later found that certain reactions in the hydrogen atom's nucleus produced large amounts of energy. Aware that stars are made mostly of hydrogen, Bethe showed that even if a star burned millions of tons of its mass every second, its loss of energy over a long period would hardly be measurable. Born in Germany in 1906, Bethe immigrated to the U.S. in 1935. By 1938 he developed his star theory. Working on the atomic bomb project at Los Alamos, Bethe helped disclose the danger of radioactive fallout, and understanding the bomb's power, he lectured against nuclear warfare and helped negotiate the 1963 partial test ban treaty between the U.S. and Soviet Union. Bethe was honored many times for his work.

Bloch, Felix. While developing a way to measure the magnetism of atomic nuclei, Felix Bloch made possible a new method of chemical analysis—called nuclear magnetic resonance—and a way to measure small variations in the earth's magnetic field. For his work, he and E. M. Purcell, who made similar discoveries independently, won the 1952 Nobel Prize for physics. Born in Switzerland in 1905, Bloch studied to be an engineer, later switched to physics, and became a professor in Germany in 1932. With Hitler's rise to power, Bloch fled to America in 1933 and became a citizen in 1939. During World War II, he served in the Manhattan Project, helping to produce the first atomic bomb, and later on a radar project that suggested to him a method for studying nuclear magnetism. In 1954 and 1955 he was appointed first director of CERN, international nuclear research laboratory in Switzerland.

Bloch, Konrad E. For discovering how the human body uses cholesterol, a vital waxlike substance needed by all animal and human cells, Konrad Bloch shared the 1964 Nobel Prize for physiology and medicine. Bloch observed that cholesterol, found mostly in fats, nerve tissue, blood, and dairy products, performs many important functions. He demonstrated that the cholesterol in such hormones as cortisone aids the body in absorbing fats and keeps cell plasma, the fluid part of cells, from changing. Born in 1912 in Germany, Bloch studied chemistry in Munich, immigrated to America from Nazi Germany in 1936, and became a U.S. citizen eight years later. After receiving a Ph.D. in biochemistry from Columbia University, he taught at the University of Chicago and later at Columbia. Bloch joined Harvard as a professor of biochemistry and was elected to the National Academy of Sciences in 1956.

Walter Brattain   **Wallace Brode**   **Harrison Brown**

Brattain, Walter. With his associates, Walter Brattain won the 1956 Nobel Prize in physics for inventing the tiny transistor which improved the design and performance of electronic devices, including radios, television sets, and hearing aids. Brattain's point contact transistor controlled the flow of electrical current, replaced bulky vacuum tubes, and improved hearing reception. Born in 1902, Brattain received his Ph.D. from the University of Minnesota in 1929.

Brode, Wallace R. While experimenting with chemical dye colorings, 20th century chemist Wallace Brode developed precision instruments enabling scientists to observe the wavelengths of colors. Brode later discovered that wavelengths of light revealed additional scientific knowledge about the molecular structure of dyes and other chemical substances. He also developed colorful take-a-part models to teach the construction of molecules. Born in 1900 in Washington, Brode earned his Ph.D. from the University of Illinois. Beginning in 1928, Brode taught chemistry at Ohio State University until his appointment in 1948 as associate director of the U.S. National Bureau of Standards. In 1958 he was elected president of the American Association for the Advancement of Science. Brode's book, *Chemical Spectroscopy*, was one of the first on that subject. At one time a state department adviser, he died in 1974.

That year he began work in a telephone company's research laboratory. A defense researcher during World War II, he later joined John Bardeen and William Shockley in constructing the transistor, a small device controlling the flow of electric current. Together they developed a working model in 1947 and perfected it within a few years, enabling manufacturers to produce transistors inexpensively. Brattain also did research on magnetism.

Brown, Harrison. The earth's age, the history of the solar system, and man's use of science and technology were problems geochemist Harrison Brown worked to solve in the mid-1900s. Born in Wyoming in 1917, Brown graduated from Johns Hopkins and supervised U.S. plutonium research in World War II. He joined California Institute of Technology, becoming professor of science and government in 1967. Brown developed methods to measure accurately the age and composition of rocks. Comparing properties of lead on earth to lead in meteors, he estimated the earth's age at 4.5 billion years. Brown also used his methods to classify planets by age and chemical properties, helping scientists construct a theory of the universe. He wrote many books about the humane uses of science and coauthored a proposal in 1960 which led to the formation of the Arms Control and Disarmament Agency.

Melvin Calvin   **Owen Chamberlain**   **Catherine Chen**

Calvin, Melvin. For unlocking the mysterious process through which green plants change poisonous carbon dioxide in the air into breathable oxygen, biochemist Melvin Calvin was awarded the 1961 Nobel Prize for chemistry. Calvin's work provided the first reasonable explanation of the vital process called photosynthesis. By feeding living plants radioactive carbon dioxide, Calvin's researchers traced rapid chemical changes occurring within plant cells.

Chamberlain, Owen. For demonstrating that a particle of matter called an antiproton exists, American physicist Owen Chamberlain shared with Emilio Segre a Nobel Prize in 1959. Using the newly built Bevatron accelerator, Chamberlain in his experiments bombarded stationary copper neutrons with high-energy protons producing more massive particles which later were identified as antiprotons. Born in San Francisco in 1920, the son of a radiologist, Chamberlain received a bachelor's degree in science at Dartmouth in 1941. He interrupted graduate studies to work on the Manhattan atomic bomb project from 1942 to 1946. Chamberlain received a doctor's degree from the University of Chicago in 1949, where he studied under Enrico Fermi. He became a professor of physics in 1958 at the University of California at Berkeley and was elected to the National Academy of Sciences.

Calvin's breakthrough was considered of major importance since photosynthesis provides nutritious foods for animals and humans and creates the necessary oxygen to sustain life. Since only living plants could be used, his breakthrough of the photosynthesis process was slow and painstaking. Born in Minnesota in 1911, Calvin earned his Ph.D. at the University of Minnesota and joined the University of California at Berkeley in 1937.

Chen, Catherine S. H. Research scientist and chemist Catherine Chen, beginning in 1955, developed many new and improved plastics and textiles used throughout American homes and industries. By developing the fiber polyprophylene in 1960, she originated a synthetic material which could be used in clothing and furniture upholstery. The new materials had long wearability and stain resistant properties. Born in Chungking, China in 1925, Catherine Chen earned her Ph.D. from the Brooklyn Polytechnical Institute in 1955. After serving at Columbia University, she became a research scientist for a chemical manufacturer. During the 1960s and early 70s, she continued to develop new products, including photo-glue and an industrial adhesive used in the building and construction trades. Much of Catherine Chen's work laid the groundwork for further improvements in the use of plastics and textiles.

Seymour S. Cohen   James B. Conant   Carl F. and Gerty R. Cori

Cohen, Seymour S. A pioneering scientist who furthered the study of viruses, biochemist Seymour Cohen in the 1950s helped reveal how viruses, by taking control of healthy cells, cause disease. Born in 1917 in New York, Cohen received his Ph.D. in 1941 from Columbia University. His first assignment was as a researcher on plant viruses. Cohen organized the first systematic method to determine how viruses use biochemicals to multiply and kill cells in the human body. The discovery that certain cells and viruses were easier to follow than others, led other researchers to further discoveries. Cohen's studies of "foods" used by viruses revealed that some biochemicals slow virus growth. His major discovery—that a virus can cause a cell to produce a chemical required for the growth of the virus—won him a medal from the American Association for the Advancement of Science in 1955.

Conant, James B. Scientist, educator, and diplomat whose work for the government during World War II led to the development of the atomic bomb, James Conant recognized the need for greater understanding between science and education and worked untiringly for his idea in the 1950s and 60s. An outstanding researcher in organic chemistry at Harvard in the 1920s, Conant, born in Massachusetts in 1893, investigated and wrote about the structure of chlorophyll in plants and hemoglobin in blood. Serving as president of Harvard from 1933 to 1953, he helped found the National Science Foundation after World War II and was a member of the Atomic Energy Commission. Appointed ambassador to Germany in the 1950s, he returned to the United States in 1957 to undertake a study of American high schools. His notable books on education include *Shaping Educational Policy* (1964).

Cori: Carl F. and Gerty R. For discovering how the human body converts food into energy, a husband and wife research team—Carl and Gerty Radnitz Cori—was awarded the Nobel Prize for medicine and physiology in 1947. The Coris' investigation showed that glycogen (a starch), the carbohydrate drawn from food, breaks down into a series of phosphate compounds instead of into glucose (sugar) molecules. This indirect process allows the body to make the conversion with little loss of energy. They also isolated a previously unknown compound from the muscle tissue where the conversion of glucose to energy takes place. This substance, glucose-1-phosphate, was named Coriester in their honor. Both Coris were born in 1896 in Prague, Czechoslovakia. After meeting at school, they both obtained medical degrees and were married in 1920. In 1922 they immigrated to the United States.

Michael De Bakey

Rene Jules Dubos

De Bakey, Michael. Credited with developing surgical practices that saved thousands of lives in the mid-1900s, heart surgeon and medical researcher Michael De Bakey pioneered open-heart surgery, the use of artificial organs, and heart transplants. In the 1930s he helped develop the first dependable heart-lung machine, which allowed surgeons to stop the heart while performing open-heart surgery. De Bakey also led a research team which invented a mechanical heart pump to supply blood to the body. He became one of the first surgeons to transplant blood vessels and helped develop artificial dacron tubes that could be grafted into the body to replace diseased vessels.

Born in Louisiana in 1908, De Bakey earned his medical degree from Tulane University in 1932. After studying surgery in the United States and Europe, he joined the medical faculty of Tulane in 1937. In 1948 he was chosen chairman of the Department of Surgery at Baylor University. In 1963, he became the first surgeon to successfully implant a temporary artificial heart pump in a patient. The pump allowed the patient's heart to heal until it was able to function normally. De Bakey received many honors and awards for his outstanding medical achievements, including the Albert Lasker Award for Clinical Research in 1963. Beginning in the late 1960s, De Bakey turned to solving the problems of organ transplants and their acceptance or rejection by the human body. Author of many books and professional papers, he strongly supported cooperative research programs with foreign surgeons.

Dubos, Rene Jules. Developer of the first antibiotic drug in 1939, microbiologist Rene Dubos also originated techniques that helped other scientists discover penicillin and later "miracle" drugs which proved effective against many diseases. Dubos's own discovery, tyrothricin, while effective against many disease-causing bacteria, produced too many side effects for popular use. Born in France in 1901, Dubos came to the U.S. in 1924 and received his Ph.D. from Rutgers University in 1927. Later while specializing in microbiology at the Rockefeller Institute, Dubos found that disease bacteria could not survive in soil. After many experiments, he discovered that microbes found in the soil produced an antibiotic that could destroy bacteria. From his findings, Dubos was able to isolate the antibiotic microbes and produce a drug that killed specific bacteria. Dubos later did research on tuberculosis.

Vincent Du Vigneaud

John Franklin Enders

Du Vigneaud, Vincent. The first man to synthesize a protein, a basic element of the body, Vincent Du Vigneaud in 1954 put together an exact chemical duplicate of the pituitary gland hormone oxytocin. It was a small protein molecule of only eight amino acids. Du Vigneaud's synthetic hormone caused the same reaction within the human body as the natural hormone. His work, which won him the Nobel Prize for chemistry in 1955, opened the way for the synthetic construction of other proteins. Born in 1901 in Chicago, Du Vigneaud obtained his Ph. D. from the University of Rochester in 1927. Interested in the structure of amino acids, he discovered how the body alters one chemical compound into another closely related compound until a complete molecule is formed. In 1942, Du Vigneaud determined the structure of the body chemical compound biotin, a vitamin.

Enders, John Franklin. Member of a research team whose discoveries in the cultivation of viruses later made possible a vaccine that saved thousands from infantile paralysis, microbiologist John Enders shared the 1954 Nobel Prize in physiology and medicine. Knowledge of the discoveries made by Enders and his co-workers, F.C. Robbins and T.H. Weller, with whom Enders shared the prize, later helped Jonas Salk develop the vaccine that proved to be effective against poliomyelitis. Born in 1897 in Connecticut, Enders received a Ph.D. in bacteriology and immunology from Harvard in 1930. After serving as a navy pilot in World War II, Enders began the study of tuberculosis, bacterial infections, and resistance to bacterial diseases. He also studied the viral diseases of measles, influenza, and mumps. Named chief of the research department at Boston's Children's Hospital, he led the team of scientists that in 1948 succeeded in growing the poliomyelitis virus in cultures of tissues.

The polio virus isolated by the Enders team was tested on animals and later on tissue obtained from operations on children and adults. After thousands of experiments on viruses including those cultivated by Enders, Salk in 1952 developed the first effective poliomyelitis vaccine that later other scientists refined for mass use. The discoveries made by Enders and his team made possible new methods of diagnosis and the isolation of many viruses. The research team isolated the virus of measles in 1954 and paved the way for a live measles vaccine used successfully throughout the world.

Karl August Folkers   **Raymond Fuoss**   **Murray Gell-Mann**

Folkers, Karl August. Heading the group that isolated vitamin B_{12} in 1948, biochemist Karl Folkers through his work was able to give new hope to patients suffering from harmful pernicious anemia. This discovery along with his work on antibiotics ranked as major contributions to medicine. Born in 1906 in Illinois, Folkers was determined to make chemistry his lifework. Earning his Ph.D. from the University of Wisconsin in 1931, he became associated with a drug firm and in 1956 was appointed director of biochemical research. Named president of a research institute in 1963, Folkers was later appointed professor of chemistry at Stanford University and lecturer in vitamin chemistry at the University of California. Winner of many scientific awards, Folkers received the Presidential Certificate of Merit in 1948 for his work during World War II in furthering research for military needs.

Fuoss, Raymond. Pioneering the application of electric fields to chemical systems to determine their molecular structures, Raymond Fuoss made valuable research contributions in the field of chemistry during the 20th century. Born in 1905 in Pennsylvania, Fuoss graduated in 1925 from Harvard and in 1932 received his Ph.D. from Brown University, where he remained until 1933 as assistant professor for research. In 1935 he received the American Chemical Society Award for "a theory of electrolytic solutions applicable to solvent media." Fuoss's theory included an analysis of the composition of liquid molecular structures and led to an understanding of the processes of transition within them. Fuoss worked on the electrical properties of plastic compositions for private industry until 1945, when he was appointed Sterling Professor of Chemistry at Yale University. Many citations honor his research.

Gell-Mann, Murray. Regarded by some scientists as a successor to physicist Albert Einstein, Murray Gell-Mann received the Nobel Prize for physics in 1969. His outstanding research produced the significant finding that certain elementary particles found in the atomic nucleus have an interaction quality called "strangeness," and that the subatomic particles keep the "strangeness" in strong interactions. Gell-Mann's law of conservation of strangeness helped explain the odd behavior of the particles to physicists. Born in New York in 1929, Gell-Mann as a boy found schoolwork dull. He entered Yale at the age of 15. He first grew enthusiastic about the study of physics while working on his Ph.D. degree at Massachusetts Institute of Technology. In 1956, at the age of 26, Gell-Mann became a full professor at the California Institute of Technology. Gell-Mann was elected to the National Academy of Sciences in 1960.

William Giauque   **Donald Glaser**   **Robert Hofstadter**

Giauque, William. Opening up the region of ultimate cold for intensive study, chemist William Giauque won the 1949 Nobel Prize in chemistry for devising a way to decrease temperature close to absolute zero. Giauque found that magnetic salts, surrounding liquid helium and falling out of alignment when the magnetic field is removed, would absorb heat and the temperature of the helium would drop even further. Born in Canada in 1895, Giauque received a Ph.D. from the University of California, where he joined the faculty in 1922 and further researched the field of low temperatures. Giauque was responsible in 1961 for the shift from oxygen-16 to carbon-12 as the standard for atomic weight. This followed his earlier discovery that the oxygen-16 isotope differs slightly between its physical and chemical atomic weights. Giauque was elected to the National Academy of Sciences in 1936.

Glaser, Donald. A method of recording rare or short-lived nuclear events was found in 1952 when physicist Donald Glaser constructed his first "bubble chamber" used to track high-energy, subatomic particles. Awarded the Nobel Prize in physics in 1960 for his discovery, Glaser used liquid hydrogen to boil around incoming ions from huge atomic accelerators. Glaser found that drops of gas produced tracks in a bubble chamber which were quickly slowed and formed shorter and more highly curved paths. He found also that the tracks could be easily photographed in the liquid hydrogen. Born in Ohio in 1926, Glaser graduated from Case Institute in 1946 and earned a Ph.D. at the California Institute of Technology in 1949. After research at the University of Michigan, he became professor at the University of California. In 1962 Glaser was elected to the National Academy of Sciences.

Hofstadter, Robert. By increasing the list of known subatomic particles during the 1960s and placing them in a fundamental order, physicist Robert Hofstadter added to modern man's understanding of the atom. Born in 1915 in New York, Hofstadter received his Ph.D. degree from Princeton University in 1938. During World War II, he helped develop a proximity fuse for the military services. Appointed professor of physics at Stanford University in 1950, Hofstadter became chairman of the physics department in 1954. Using the large linear accelerator at Stanford to "shoot" atomic particles in a straight line, Hofstadter studied the scattering effects imposed on high-energy electrons by atomic nuclei. In 1960 Hofstadter found heavier, short-lived mesons within the nucleus of the atom and in 1961 shared the Nobel Prize in physics. Hofstadter continued to study the structure of the atom.

Percy Lavon Julian

Arthur Kornberg

Julian, Percy Lavon. Despite the lack of opportunity for black scientists in the field of research chemistry, Percy Julian, grandson of a slave, won worldwide recognition in the late 1930s for his discovery of an inexpensive way of manufacturing cortisone, a drug used in the treatment of many diseases. Credited with the discovery of physostigmine, a drug used in treating glaucoma, Julian became a leading medical research authority in the U.S.

Born in Alabama in 1899, Julian worked his way through DePauw University by serving as a waiter, and he graduated first in his class in 1920. Julian attended the graduate schools of Fisk and Harvard universities and in 1931 earned a Ph.D. degree from the University of Vienna. Julian taught chemistry at Howard and DePauw universities before accepting a position as director of research for a Chicago chemical company in 1936. During the next 17 years, he and a staff of fifty associates patented 42 chemical discoveries, mostly derived from soybeans. Opening his own laboratory in 1954, Julian concentrated on the research of sterols from soybean oil and other plants. Prior to Julian's work, the solid unsaturated sterols were derived at great cost from the tissues of plants and animals. In creating inexpensive soya sterols, Julian in the early 1950s enabled cortisone to be widely distributed at low cost to arthritic sufferers. Other Julian discoveries included a soya protein for use in coating paper and the chemical base for a foam fire extinguisher used by the U.S. Navy during World War II. He died in 1975.

Kornberg, Arthur. Following the DNA theory, advanced by scientists Watson and Crick in 1953, of how cells in living organisms are formed and reproduce themselves, biochemist Arthur Kornberg separated an enzyme in his laboratory in 1956 that, when combined with other elements in a living cell, formed a part of the DNA (deoxy ribonucleic acid) chain. For his pioneering work, Kornberg shared the Nobel Prize for medicine in 1959. His work in 1956 was a major breakthrough in the study of living organisms. In 1967 he and his associates were able to produce a chemical strand of the molecule (DNA) that was able to reproduce itself as in living organisms.

Kornberg was born in 1918 in Brooklyn and graduated from the College of the City of New York in 1937. He received his M.D. degree from the University of Rochester in 1941 and began research on body fluid enzymes necessary to keep human cells functioning. Following military service in World War II, Kornberg joined the staff of the National Institute of Health and served as section chief of the enzymes and metabolism division from 1947 to 1951. Later Kornberg was appointed director of the Department of Microbiology at Washington University School of Medicine. In 1957 he produced the first molecules of DNA. In 1959 Kornberg was named chairman of the department of biochemistry at the Stanford University School of Medicine. In 1967 he announced his success in creating a reproducing active molecule of artificial DNA. Kornberg published *Enzymatic Synthesis of DNA* in 1962.

Joshua Lederberg   **Tsung-Dao Lee**   **Willard F. Libby**

Lederberg, Joshua. The 1958 Nobel Prize in medicine was shared by geneticist Joshua Lederberg for his discoveries in bacterial heredity. Lederberg found that the genetic material in bacteria could be intermingled through sexual reproduction, thus producing different strains of bacteria. With Lederberg's discovery, geneticists could study an organism with rapid growth and a simple structure. Born in 1925 in New Jersey, Lederberg graduated from Columbia College in 1944 and received his Ph.D. in microbiology from Yale in 1948. He joined the faculty of the University of Wisconsin in 1950 and accepted the post of chairman of the genetics department at Stanford University in 1959. Lederberg also showed how a bacterial virus could carry hereditary material from one cell to another, a process called transduction. Scientists believed his work could lead to controlling all virus diseases.

Lee, Tsung-Dao. A new era in the science of physics was opened when Tsung-Dao Lee and Chen Ning Yang in 1956 disproved the long-held theory that nature always maintains a perfect balance or parity between interacting particles. For their discovery—that the emissions from weak subatomic interactions many times "preferred" to become one type rather than another—Lee and Yang in 1957 became the first Chinese-Americans to win a Nobel Prize. Scientists working from their new theories began to study whether nature is really neutral or whether the laws of nature prefer a certain goal. Lee was born in China in 1926 and met Yang while studying in China in 1945. Awarded a fellowship, Lee moved to the United States and received his Ph.D. from the University of Chicago in 1950. Lee taught at Columbia University and moved to Princeton University in 1960.

Libby, Willard F. Radiocarbon dating—a process of determining the age of fossils by measuring the amount of isotope carbon 14 in a sample—was discovered by physicist Willard Libby in 1949. It led to his winning the Nobel Prize in chemistry in 1960. Born in Colorado in 1908, Libby received his Ph.D. at the University of California at Berkeley in 1933 and joined the faculty. During World War II, he worked on the atomic bomb project and in 1945 joined the University of Chicago's Institute of Nuclear Studies. In developing his radiocarbon dating process four years later, Libby first measured the faint radioactivity in living matter. Later, Libby discovered the method for determining the exact age of ancient organic matter by measuring its amount of carbon 14. Libby served on the Atomic Energy Commission and the faculty of the University of California at Los Angeles.

Fritz A. Lipmann

Edwin McMillan

Lipmann, Fritz A. For isolating and identifying a vital biological element in the body-building process, biochemist Fritz Lipmann was awarded the Nobel Prize in medicine in 1953. Lipmann demonstrated that an element called "coenzyme A" is necessary for the conversion of most foods into energy in the human body. Born in 1899 in Germany, Lipmann received degrees in medicine and chemistry at the University of Berlin. He came to the U.S.

from Denmark in 1931 on a fellowship and returned to Denmark in 1932. He left Denmark again in 1939 to return to America and became a research fellow at Cornell University. In 1941 he became senior biochemist at the Massachusetts General Hospital and in 1949 was named professor of biological chemistry at Harvard Medical School. In 1957 Lipmann became a professor at the Rockefeller Institute for Medical Research in New York City.

McMillan, Edwin. Discovering the radioactive element neptunium that led to creation of the nuclear energy material plutonium, Edwin McMillan shared the 1951 Nobel Prize for chemistry with Glenn Seaborg, discoverer of plutonium. McMillan was experimenting in 1940 with atomic fission when he determined that a new element, number 93, was produced in tiny amounts by a reaction that occurred when uranium was exposed to neutron beams from a circular accelerator known as a cyclotron. Since uranium had been named for the planet Uranus, McMillan called the newly discovered element neptunium after Neptune, the planet beyond Uranus.

McMillan was also known for his invention of the synchrocyclotron. In the early 1940s, it was found that when particles are speeded

to great velocity by cyclotrons, the mass of the particles increases noticeably, preventing the continuing pushes that would speed them even faster. Finding that cyclotrons had reached their limits, McMillan in 1945 devised an accelerator called a synchrocyclotron, which adjusted the pushes given to the particles by the electric field and gave them increased velocity. During the 1960s, synchrocyclotrons opened new secrets of the atom to scientists. Born in 1907 in California, McMillan graduated from the California Institute of Technology in 1928 and obtained his Ph.D. at Princeton in 1932. He helped develop radar, sonar, and atomic weapons during World War II. McMillan joined the faculty at the University of California at Berkeley in 1946.

Theodore H. Maiman

Erwin Mueller

Maiman, Theodore H. A physicist who worked his way through college by repairing electrical appliances, Theodore Maiman won wide acclaim in the 1960s for inventing and developing the laser, a device that created "coherent light" by producing a powerful beam with the possibility of rising to temperatures of thousands of degrees. He called it "laser" by combining the first letters of: light amplification by stimulated emission of radiation. Earlier Maiman had developed an improved maser, a device that generates radio waves, which was more compact and powerful than older versions and operated at a higher temperature.

Born in 1927 in California, Maiman was inspired to follow a career in science by his father, an electrical engineer. After graduating from the University of Colorado in 1949, Maiman received his Ph.D. in physics at Stanford University in 1955. To create his improved maser, he used a carefully processed ruby. Other scientists had considered using the ruby to focus and concentrate light in a laser, but most of their results were inefficient; Maiman continued to experiment until he created a "lens" that was composed of a highly polished ruby cylinder with silver coating on each end. In 1960, Maiman flashed a bright light into the device and produced the first laser beam. Maiman founded a company in 1962 to improve and manufacture lasers. For his achievement, Maiman received awards from the Franklin Institute in 1962 and the American Physical Society. He was presented the Hertz Foundation Award in 1966.

Mueller, Erwin. By inventing a microscope in 1936 that enlarges objects to a million times their actual size, physicist Erwin Mueller enabled scientists for the first time to see individual atoms—the smallest units of matter. Mueller's invention definitely proved the existence of atoms, a theory that had been proposed nearly 2,400 years before by Democritus, an early Greek philosopher, and long ridiculed by many men of science. Called a field-emission microscope, Mueller's development uses a tiny needle tip that sends electrons or ions against a fluorescent screen. The screen, many thousands of times bigger than the tip, projects a greatly enlarged image of the tip so that individual atoms can be seen. Magnifications of up to a million times are possible.

Born in 1911 in Germany, Mueller graduated in 1935 from the Technical University at Berlin. After working in Berlin for seventeen years, he came to America in 1952 and became physics professor at Pennsylvania State University. Mueller's perfection of the field-emission microscope was completed in 1936, but for some time its use was limited to high-melting alloys or metals. It has since proved valuable in studying the amounts of gas absorbed by surfaces of solids and detecting flaws in crystals. In a later development, Mueller attached to his microscope a measuring device called a mass spectrometer, which permits identification of individual atoms as they are extracted from the top by the use of high voltage and times their speed along the spectrometer tube. Mueller became a United States citizen in 1962.

Robert S. Mulliken

Marshall W. Nirenberg

Mulliken, Robert S. After proposing a new theory on how atoms are held together in a molecule, Robert Mulliken was awarded the Nobel Prize in chemistry in 1966 for his work in molecular interaction. Until then, scientists had believed that each atom in a molecule remained an independent unit. In 1928 Mulliken stated in his "molecular-orbital" theory that atoms merge and form a new entity. Born in 1896, he was a high school student when he began proofreading chemistry textbooks written by his father. Mulliken received his Ph.D. in 1921 at the University of Chicago, where he became associate professor of physics in 1928, full professor in 1931, and distinguished service professor in 1961. During World War II, Mulliken was director of information for the plutonium project at the University of Chicago. Mulliken was the first to program computer formulas for molecular research.

Nirenberg, Marshall W. By discovering how protein organic compounds called amino acids—the building blocks of life—are constructed in living cells, biochemist Marshall Nirenberg made a major advance in understanding the nature of life. For his work, he shared the 1968 Nobel Prize for medicine and physiology. Born in New York City in 1927, Nirenberg was raised in Florida, where he became interested in biochemistry at the University of Florida. He received his Ph.D. from the University of Michigan in 1957. Nirenberg joined the National Institute of Health (NIH) as a postdoctoral fellow, and in 1962 he became chief of the Laboratory of Biochemical Genetics of the NIH National Heart Institute.

From the work of other scientists, Nirenberg knew that living cells transfer information about their chemical composition to new cells by means of two chemicals, named deoxyribonucleic acid (DNA) and ribonucleic acid (RNA), which direct amino acids into the protein that forms new cells. In 1961 Nirenberg created RNA artificially and added it to a batch of amino acids. To each amino acid in turn he added a small amount of radioactive carbon 14. The carbon 14, by giving off radioactivity, showed Nirenberg which amino acid was being directed into protein by the artificial RNA and enabled him to identify it precisely. By 1962 Nirenberg and his assistants had identified 15 additional combinations of amino acids and RNA. Nirenberg received various awards, including the National Medal of Science in 1965.

John H. Northrop   **Severo Ochoa**   **John A. O'Keefe**

Northrop, John H. For helping reveal the chemical structure of three enzymes that control digestion and increasing knowledge of the human body, biochemist John Northrop shared the 1946 Nobel Prize in chemistry. Before Northrop's research, scientists believed that enzymes helped regulate body processes but knew nothing about their chemical composition. Between 1930 and 1935, Northrop discovered the protein nature of the enzymes pepsin, trypsin, and chymotrypsin and led the way to further research on the role of proteins in digestion. Suspecting that viruses and enzymes have the same general chemical structures, Northrop was the first to analyze the chemical makeup of a virus. Northrop was born in New York in 1891. He received his Ph.D. from Columbia University in 1915, then served on the staff of the Rockefeller Institute for Medical Research from 1916 until 1961.

Ochoa, Severo. By artificially producing ribonucleic acid (RNA), a basic part of all living cells, in his laboratory in 1955, biochemist Severo Ochoa made significant progress toward uncovering the secrets of life's beginning. For his work, Ochoa shared the 1959 Nobel Prize in medicine and physiology. Ochoa was born in Spain in 1905 and obtained his M.D. degree in Madrid in 1929. He arrived in the United States in 1940 and soon joined the faculty of New York University's College of Medicine, becoming chairman of its biochemistry department in 1954. Ochoa knew that living creatures produce nucleic acids through interactions of enzymes (body proteins) and units called nucleotides. In his laboratory, he permitted an enzyme from a strain of bacteria to react with nucleotides. The result was the formation of artificial particles of RNA. Ochoa was elected to the National Academy of Sciences in 1957.

O'Keefe, John A. Closely checking movements in space of the American man-made satellite *Vanguard I*, physicist John O'Keefe discovered in 1960 that the earth is not a perfect globe, but slightly pear-shaped. Smaller than earlier satellites at only three pounds, *Vanguard I*, launched in 1958, was placed farther out in space, where it could orbit longer because of less friction from the surrounding atmosphere. As the satellite orbited the earth, O'Keefe detected motions caused by differing pulls of gravity from high and low spots on the ground. He learned that the earth has a 50-foot-greater bulge north of the equator than it does to the south, and that the North Pole is 100 feet closer to the center of the earth than is the South Pole. Born in 1916 in Massachusetts, O'Keefe graduated from Harvard in 1937. He joined the National Aeronautics and Space Administration in 1960.

Linus Pauling

Pauling, Linus. The first to win two unshared Nobel Prizes in different fields of study, chemist Linus Pauling received the 1954 Nobel Prize in chemistry for work on the structures of molecules and the 1962 Nobel Peace Prize. Studying in Europe in 1926-27, Pauling worked with leading physicists Summerfield, Bohr, and Schroedinger and became interested in their new scientific theory of quantum mechanics, according to which atoms are composed of discontinuous units or bits of energy that can never be exact. Pauling's early work led him to consider the forces that hold a molecule together—the chemical bonds between its atoms. He first explored the crystalline structures of metals and compounds by means of x-rays and then advanced to the more complex molecules that are found in living systems.

In the late 1920s, applying the new quantum (or wave) mechanics, he advanced his "resonance" theory of the structures of certain molecules. Benzene, for example—whose structure could not be explained by any one pattern of conventional bonds—was described by Pauling quantum-mechanically as "resonating," or shifting between several conventional bond structures, which it holds in equilibrium. Turning to protein research, he studied the structures of the key components of proteins, including peptides and amino acids, again by using x-rays. In 1951 he announced that protein molecules are arranged in helices—spiral staircase forms.

Pauling was born in Oregon in 1901, the son of a druggist. He graduated from Oregon State College in 1922 and received his Ph.D. from California Institute of Technology in 1925, where he taught for most of his life. In 1937 he was named chairman of the Department of Chemistry and director of the university laboratories. After World War II, Pauling fought to halt all test explosions of nuclear weapons and to achieve worldwide nuclear disarmament. In 1958 he wrote *No More War!* and continued to warn about the threat to people caused by radioactive fallout from atomic weapons. From 1964 to 1969 he was associated with the Center for the Study of Democratic Institutions.

Pauling's resonance theory led to the development of many new drugs, plastics, and synthetic fibers. His classic text *The Nature of the Chemical Bond* (1939) influenced the study of advanced chemistry. Pauling's theory of protein structure helped in the later discovery of DNA (the carrier of genes)—a breakthrough in genetics and a step toward gaining accurate understanding of the very basis of life.

Gregory Pincus

Kenneth S. Pitzer

Pincus, Gregory. Experimenting in studies of hormones (body chemicals that control organ functions), biologist Gregory Pincus helped develop the first oral birth-control pill in the 1950s. Pincus discovered that the hormone progesterone acts in the body to prevent twin births and that when additional amounts are consumed by the female, human conception is prevented altogether. This discovery led to the development, with M. C. Chang, of an artificial progesterone that became popularly known as "the Pill." Pincus also helped to perfect a method for quick-freezing living male sex cells and preserving them alive for many years.

Pincus was born in New Jersey in 1903 and received his Sc.D. from Harvard in 1927. While teaching at Harvard and Clark universities, he experimented with egg cells taken from female rabbits. In one experiment he succeeded in uniting, in a test tube, male cells with the female cells. Pincus later experimented without the use of male sex cells, to stimulate the development of an egg by using hormones, salt solutions, heat, and pin pricks. He was able to cause the cells to divide and grow, and by surgically implanting the egg within a mother, he produced the virgin birth of a baby rabbit. In 1944 Pincus joined the Worcester Foundation for Experimental Biology, where he continued his studies of hormones and developed the progesterone hormone pill. Perfected by several drug laboratories, the pill was field tested under Pincus's supervision in 1956 and licensed for use in 1960. In the late 1960s Pincus experimented on a simpler form of birth-control pill.

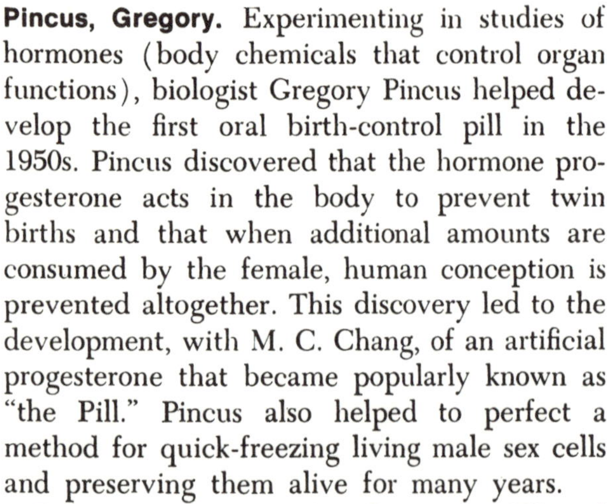

Pitzer, Kenneth S. To make the chemical lab worker's job easier, Kenneth Pitzer in the mid-20th century turned complicated theories about the structure of atoms into approximations that predict the directions and rates of laboratory reactions at different temperatures. Hydrocarbons, one group of chemicals for which he made such calculations, are found in gasoline, vaseline, and rubber. Pitzer was born in California in 1914 and received his Ph.D. in 1937 from the University of California, where he taught for 24 years, finally becoming dean of the college of chemistry. In 1961 he became president of Rice University. Pitzer also worked as research director for the Atomic Energy Commission and in 1964 served on the President's Science Advisory Committee. Pitzer was elected in 1949 to the National Academy of Sciences and awarded the Lewis Medal of the American Chemical Society in 1965.

Edward M. Purcell

Isidor I. Rabi

Purcell, Edward M. For his use of magnetism as a method of measuring nuclear and molecular properties, Edward Purcell shared the 1952 Nobel Prize for physics. Born in 1912 in Illinois, he attended Purdue and received his Ph.D. at Harvard in 1938. During World War II, Purcell conducted research on radar at the Massachusetts Institute of Technology and, at night, performed nuclear experiments, passing atomic particles through magnetic fields and measuring the results. He found that the magnetic field rose and fell, revealing a top-like wobbling rotation of the particles. In 1946 he joined the Harvard faculty. Purcell found that a particle reacts differently to a magnetic field when located in a molecule or crystal— a fact that illuminates the nature of chemical bonding. In 1951 Purcell studied radio astronomy and, he detected the microwaves emitted by neutral hydrogen in empty space.

Rabi, Isidor I. By passing beams of atoms and molecules through a series of magnetic fields— some pulsed like radio waves—atomic physicist Isidor Rabi caused small shifts in energy within the atom and distinguished fine differences in possible energy levels. For his outstanding study, which led to development of the atomic clock and the laser (a superpowerful ray) by later scientists, Rabi was awarded the Nobel Prize for physics in 1944.

Rabi was born in Austria in 1898 and received his Ph.D. from Columbia in 1927. After studying under Europe's foremost physicists, who interested him in the atomic-beam technique, he returned to Columbia in 1929 as a faculty member. At the university he invented the resonance method that won him the Nobel Prize and used the method to measure the size and direction of the magnetic moments (sensitivities to magnetic fields) of protons, deuterons, and nuclei. During World War II, Rabi was associate director of the Radiation Laboratory at Massachusetts Institute of Technology, where he employed his beams to help in the development of radar. Deeply concerned with the social problems created by the atomic bomb, he worked on government committees, including the advisory committee for the Atomic Energy Commission. He was selected as chairman of the commission and also served on the president's Science Advisory Committee. As director of Columbia's physics department until 1963, Rabi urged further research with atom smashers. To study high-energy physics, he helped found the Brookhaven National Laboratory.

Norman F. Ramsey   **Frederick C. Robbins**   **William C. Rose**

Ramsey, Norman F. Probing the interiors of atoms and molecules, physicist Norman Ramsey in the 1950s measured their electrical and magnetic forces with unusual accuracy. Having made the first precise measurements of the tiny magnetic fields of molecules, Ramsey showed that the amount of this energy depends on the weights of their atomic nuclei. To determine this fact, Ramsey devised new techniques and instruments. Born in Washington,

Robbins, Frederick C. As one of a group of three medical scientists financed by the March of Dimes—a fund to further research—Frederick Robbins helped develop a method for growing polio virus in a test tube and was awarded a share of the 1954 Nobel Prize in physiology and medicine. The method Robbins helped develop enabled Jonas Salk to create a vaccine that immunized people from polio. Before Robbins, polio research was done mainly on monkeys. In the newer tests, kidney tissues pasted along the sides of a test tube were first bathed in nutrients, then exposed to air and to nutrients again. Polio virus could then be grown on the tissues, enabling closer study by the scientists. Born in Alabama in 1916, Robbins received his M.D. from Harvard in 1940. He was associated with Children's Hospital in Boston from 1946 to 1952 and was named professor of pediatrics at Western Reserve University in 1952.

D.C. in 1915, Ramsey received his Ph.D. degree at Columbia University in 1940. During World War II, he helped develop new types of radar, served as a science consultant to the secretary of war, and worked on the atomic bomb project. Returning to Columbia after the war, Ramsey became professor of physics in 1950. He received the U.S. Atomic Energy Commission's Ernest O. Lawrence Award in 1960 for his achievements.

Rose, William C. Studying the amino acids (the building blocks of proteins), biochemist William Rose discovered in the 1940s that nearly half of the necessary acids cannot be chemically produced by the body and are obtainable only from foods. In his studies using rats, Rose found that when a rodent's body was lacking any one of ten basic acids, it lost weight and died. In his tests on humans, Rose learned that when any one of eight acids was lacking, they became irritable, easily tired, and suffered loss of appetite; when the missing amino acid was restored, the symptoms disappeared. By gradually reducing the dosage of one acid at a time, Rose determined the exact amount the human body required for adequate nutrition. Born in South Carolina in 1887, Rose received his Ph.D. at Yale in 1911. He served at the University of Illinois as a professor of biochemistry from 1922 until his retirement in 1955.

Albert B. Sabin

Carl Sagan

Sabin, Albert B. Working to discover a treatment or cure for virus diseases, medical researcher Albert Sabin developed an effective polio vaccine in 1955 composed of a live virus that could be administered by mouth. Earlier, when a patient died from a monkey bite, Sabin discovered that a specific virus that was harmless in the animal's system proved fatal when it entered the human body. Sabin served as a medical officer during World War II and developed vaccines against dengue fever and encephalitis, diseases afflicting U.S. troops in the tropics.

Sabin was born in Poland in 1906 and immigrated to the U.S. with his family when 15. He received his M.D. in 1931 from New York University and in 1939 was appointed to the medical faculty of the University of Cincinnati and to the Children's Hospital Research Foundation. Sabin began his studies of polio in 1941, and after 23 years of research he decided that his early experiments showed sufficient evidence to attempt large-scale tests on humans. Unlike Jonas Salk's earlier polio vaccine, composed of dead viruses, Sabin's vaccine required live but extremely weak virus strains, which provided stronger immunity. Sabin first tried the vaccine on himself in 1954, then experimented with volunteer convicts. At the recommendation of the World Health Organization, successful trials were made on 6 million adults and children in Russia and 200,000 children in Mexico. Sabin's vaccine was certified for use in the United States in 1961. Afterwards Sabin concentrated his virus research on seeking an effective treatment for cancer.

Sagan, Carl. Denying the belief that the oldest microbes on earth originated from distant planets, astronomer and astrophysicist Carl Sagan proposed in the 1960s that the earth microbes arose when lightning shocked the atmosphere and produced amino acids—the building blocks of proteins. Studying the probability of life existing on other planets and how life arose on earth, he began specializing in 1961 in planetary atmospheres and surfaces. He found that the clouds of Venus produce extremely hot temperatures by trapping the heat from sunlight. He also believed that color changes on Mars—which some astronomers thought were seasonal spreading of plants—are due to the blowing of dust from the highlands. Born in New York City in 1934, Sagan received his Ph.D. in 1960 from the University of Chicago. In 1968 he was appointed director of the Laboratory for Planetary Studies at Cornell.

Jonas E. Salk

Salk, Jonas E.   Developing the most dramatic medical discovery since Edward Jenner first inoculated a child against smallpox in 1797, Jonas Salk in 1953 produced a vaccine, composed of inactive virus, to immunize youngsters and grownups against poliomyelitis, popularly called polio. Following earlier discoveries of the cultivation of viruses made by John Enders and his associates in the early 1950s, Salk furthered their research to produce his effective inactivated-virus polio vaccine.

Salk was born in New York in 1914, graduated from College of the City of New York in 1934, and received his M.D. in 1939 from New York University. An intern at Mount Sinai Hospital, he specialized in bacteriology. Awarded a fellowship in 1942 at the University of Michigan to study epidemic diseases, Salk helped develop commercial vaccines against two types of influenza viruses. He was appointed professor at the university's School of Public Health in 1946, and in 1947 Salk became an associate research professor of bacteriology at the University of Pittsburgh and director of the Virus Research Laboratory.

Sponsored by the National Foundation of Infantile Paralysis, Salk in 1949 became director at the University of Pittsburgh of a three-year project to study the polio virus. His research revealed that three strains of viruses, capable of producing polio, exist in the U.S. and that an effective vaccine would have to immunize against all three. Turning to the actual development of the polio vaccine, Salk realized that while he had to kill the polio virus used in the vaccine to make it incapable of causing polio, he had to preserve the virus's capacity to produce antibodies that would combat a polio infection. In 1952 he conducted successful tests of a Type I vaccine on children who previously suffered from polio and found they showed increased antibody levels. Extending his tests to children without a history of polio, Salk used vaccine containing inactivated viruses of all three polio types. The tests were effective, and 423,000 school children in the U.S. were given the vaccine. In a desire to mass produce the vaccine for a 1955 test, one of the manufacturers disregarded safeguards, and some of the youngsters tested became ill with polio. The error soon was corrected, and by 1961 poliomyelitis had been reduced 95% in the United States.

Salk was named professor at the University of Pittsburgh School of Medicine in 1957 and in 1963 became director of the Salk Institute for Biological Studies in California.

Julian S. Schwinger

Glenn T. Seaborg

Schwinger, Julian S. A mathematical physicist who added to the understanding of the nature of matter, Julian Schwinger shared a Nobel Prize in 1965 for his work in the field of quantum electrodynamics—the study of specific characteristics of tiny particles, including electrons. Born in New York City in 1918, Schwinger was attracted to science as a child by reading popular science magazines. He read everything on physics he could find in the public library and, when he was only eleven, read papers by English physicist Paul A. M. Dirac about electromagnetism in physics.

After graduating from high school, Schwinger entered City College of New York, where he wrote a scientific paper that won him a scholarship to Columbia. He graduated at 17 and, earning a Tyndall Traveling Fellowship, studied at Purdue, the University of Wisconsin, and Columbia. He obtained a Ph.D. at 21. In the next few years, he studied at the University of California under J. Robert Oppenheimer, taught at Purdue, helped in the development of the atomic bomb at the University of Chicago, and continued his research at the Massachusetts Institute of Technology. He joined the Harvard faculty in 1945, becoming a professor at 29. At Harvard he completed his quantum electrodynamic theory which refined the calculations based on Dirac's earlier theory. While Schwinger worked on his project, two other physicists were working independently on similar research, and all three were awarded the Nobel Prize in physics in 1965.

Seaborg, Glenn T. Inspired with an interest in chemistry and physics by a high school teacher, Glenn T. Seaborg became a nuclear chemist and shared in the scientific discovery of several elements in the 1940s and 50s that won him a 1951 Nobel Prize. His prize was awarded in chemistry, and it was shared with Edwin M. McMillan. President Kennedy appointed Seaborg chairman of the Atomic Energy Commission in 1961. Born in a mining town on the Upper Peninsula of Michigan in 1912, Seaborg moved to California with his family in 1922. In his senior year at the University of California, Seaborg changed his program to specialize in chemistry. After obtaining a Ph.D. at Berkeley in 1937, he became a research associate, and in 1940 he joined McMillan, who had produced the first synthetic element. Together they produced plutonium (94).

Seaborg moved in 1942 to the Manhattan atomic bomb project at the University of Chicago to continue plutonium research. He helped isolate a nuclear fuel, uranium 233, and discovered two new elements, americium (95) and curium (96). After his return to Berkeley in 1946, he helped discover six more elements: berkelium (97) in 1949, californium (98) in 1950, einsteinium (99) in 1942, fermium (100) in 1953, mendelevium (101) in 1955, and nobelium (102) in 1958. He became director of the Lawrence Radiation Laboratory at Berkeley in 1954 and in 1958 became chancellor of the University of California at Berkeley. Seaborg served as chairman of the Atomic Energy Commission until 1971.

William Shockley   **Albert Szent-Györgyi**   **Edward L. Tatum**

Shockley, William. For research leading to the invention of the transistor—an electronic device replacing the vacuum tube, William Shockley shared the Nobel Prize for physics in 1956 with his colleagues W. H. Brattain and John Bardeen. The three men began their search in 1946 for a device that would make radios and other electronic devices more efficient. In 1948 Shockley found that the element germanium could be used for better control of the flow of electric current. Within a few years, transistors containing germanium were used to improve the performance and reduce the size of radios, television sets, computers, and other appliances. Shockley was born in England in 1910 and received a Ph.D. from Harvard in 1936. In 1954–55 he served as research director for the U.S. Defense Department. In 1963 Shockley became professor of engineering at Stanford University.

Szent-Györgyi, Albert. For his studies on oxidation in body cells and his discovery of vitamin C—the first vitamin to be isolated in a laboratory—Albert Szent-Györgyi won a Nobel Prize in 1937. After immigrating to the U.S. in 1947, he made significant discoveries about how body chemicals make muscles work. Born in Austria-Hungary in 1893, Szent-Györgyi was wounded in World War I, and after returning to Budapest, he received his M.D. in 1917. He later studied in Germany, England, and the U.S. Noticing that some fruits turn brown when bruised while others, including lemons, oranges, and cabbages, retain their color, Szent-Györgyi found that a reducing agent contained in some plants prevents discoloration through oxidation. By isolating the reducing agent—which he named ascorbic acid—Szent-Györgyi discovered vitamin C. In the 1960s, he studied immunological capabilities of the body.

Tatum, Edward L. For his dramatic discovery that each gene in the body guides only one human chemical process, geneticist Edward Tatum pioneered in reproductive biology and shared the 1958 Nobel Prize in medicine or physiology. Using high-powered x-rays during his experiments, Tatum attacked specific intestinal bacteria and pink molds and destroyed some of the genes that were carriers of their heredity. Occasionally he found a gene that had lost its ability to create substances needed for growth. After studying the destroyed genes, Tatum concluded that each gene, by producing a specific enzyme or body chemical, directs only one special chemical process in the body. Tatum's genetic theories were soon applied to all organisms. Born in Colorado in 1909, Tatum received his Ph.D. from the University of Wisconsin. He taught at Stanford and Yale universities and the Rockefeller Institute.

Edward Teller

Teller, Edward. Designing a secret device that made the hydrogen bomb practical, physicist Edward Teller in 1952 became known as Father of the H-bomb after the first test bomb was successfully exploded on a remote Pacific island. During World War II, Teller helped in the development of the atomic bomb and from his experiments believed that it was possible to produce a more powerful thermonuclear weapon (hydrogen bomb). Teller's interest in hydrogen research began in 1935 while teaching at George Washington University in Washington, D.C. It was his studies on the vast hydrogen resources in solar energy that became the basis of his future H-bomb concepts.

Teller was born in Budapest, Hungary in 1908 and studied technology in Germany until 1928. He received a Ph.D. in physics at the University of Leipzig in Germany in 1930. Teller was awarded a Rockefeller Fellowship in 1934 to work under atomic scientist Neils Bohr. Teller immigrated to the U.S. in 1935 and taught physics at George Washington University. Following his work on the atomic bomb, Teller became a member of the Institute for Nuclear Studies at the University of Chicago in 1946. Convinced that the best insurance against war was an adequate arsenal of powerful weapons, Teller started his experiments on the H-bomb in 1949. President Truman approved the project in 1950 after it was determined other governments were capable of building their own hydrogen bomb. The bomb was bitterly attacked by opponents who believed that a weapon of such destructive power was inhuman.

Work on the U.S. H-bomb began at the Los Alamos Laboratory in New Mexico, and Teller directed the research. Severe doubts were raised as to the practical workings of the bomb, but a 1951 meeting of the Atomic Energy Commission (AEC) settled many problems, and the first H-bomb was exploded in 1952 with a force of five million tons of TNT.

After Teller directed the hydrogen bomb laboratory for the AEC, he joined the faculty of the University of California. In 1954 he was a major witness in the U.S. security hearings questioning the loyalty of J. Robert Oppenheimer, a fellow nuclear scientist. Teller testified that Oppenheimer had delayed the development of the H-bomb through lack of "moral support." His testimony was a factor in the loss of Oppenheimer's security clearance. Teller wrote *Our Nuclear Future* (with A. L. Latter) in 1958. In 1962 Teller was awarded the Atomic Energy Commission's Fermi Prize.

Joe Hin Tijo   **Charles H. Townes**   **Harold C. Urey**

Tjio, Joe Hin. Unlocking a mystery of life with his discovery in 1956 that humans have 46 chromosomes, geneticist Joe Hin Tjio advanced the study of how man developed. Since chromosomes determine and transmit hereditary characteristics, Tjio's findings opened a new era of genetics. His discovery made possible later studies in mental retardation, cancer, and criminology. Born in Indonesia in 1919, Tjio graduated from Agronomic College in Indonesia in 1941 and later directed genetics research at a Spanish experimental station. Tjio's chromosomes discovery was made at the Genetic Institute in Sweden. He was awarded a Ph.D. by the University of Colorado in 1960 and became associated with the Argonne National Laboratory in Illinois. Tjio joined the U.S. National Institutes of Health in 1959 and rose to research biologist in 1965, specializing in neoplastic diseases, including leukemia.

Townes, Charles H. After his 1953 invention of the maser, physicist Charles Townes developed the laser in 1964—a device that concentrates and intensifies a beam of ruby-colored light by stimulated emission of radiation. For his contribution, Townes shared the 1964 Nobel Prize in physics. His laser contained exact high-energy wave lengths in the visible spectrum that were capable of transmitting messages and analyzing chemicals. Born in South Carolina in 1915, Townes received his Ph.D. in 1939 from the California Institute of Technology. During World War II, he helped develop radar bombing systems. Townes's maser, an electronic amplifier that produces accurate vibrations from microwaves, was installed in 1960 as an atomic clock for the scientific measurement of time. He joined Columbia University in 1948 and in 1961 was appointed professor of physics at the Massachusetts Institute of Technology.

Urey, Harold C. For his outstanding discovery of how to produce "heavy water" needed to join hydrogen atoms together (fusion), which later made possible the powerful hydrogen bomb, Harold Urey won the 1934 Nobel Prize for chemistry. Urey found that by combining one atom of oxygen and two atoms of a heavier form of hydrogen (deuterium isotope), he was able to produce "heavy water." Born in Indiana in 1893, Urey received his Ph.D. from the University of California in 1923. He was appointed chemistry professor at Columbia in 1929 and in 1945 joined the University of Chicago. During World War II, Urey developed the process of converting gas into liquid (distillation) that helped make the atomic bomb possible, but he fought against the use of atomic and hydrogen bombs. In *Planets* (1952), he proposed a new theory of the origin of the solar system and the formation of its planets.

James Van Allen

Wernher von Braun

Van Allen, James. Reviewing information sent back to earth from the first artificial satellites in 1958, physicist James Van Allen discovered that the earth is circled by two wide belts of electrical (radiation) particles, later named the Van Allen Belts. His discovery led to major revisions in the theories about the earth's atmosphere. To further his research, Van Allen helped develop the first U.S. satellites, called Explorers. Messages sent back by *Explorer I* revealed that it met masses of electrical particles beginning about 250 miles from earth. When the count of electrical particles suddenly dropped to zero, Van Allen surmised that the satellite instruments failed to operate because of the high level of radiation. He designed a lead shield for later satellites, and the results of his research helped establish the existence of the Van Allen Belts.

Van Allen was born in Iowa in 1914 and graduated from Iowa Wesleyan College in 1935. He received a Ph.D. from the University of Iowa in 1939. Serving with the naval reserve in World War II, he developed the proximity fuse, a device directed by radio waves to explode antiaircraft shells near the target. After the war, Van Allen directed a research group at Johns Hopkins University, adapting captured German V-2 rockets for U.S. space exploration. He was appointed chairman of the physics department at the University of Iowa in 1951 and helped plan the International Geophysical Year of 1957-58, a worldwide scientific study. Van Allen was one of the founders in 1958 of the National Aeronautics and Space Administration.

Von Braun, Wernher. After directing Germany's air rocket research against the Allies in World War II, Wernher von Braun came to the U.S. and became technical director of the operational ballistic missile program for the Redstone, the rocket that placed the first U.S. artificial satellite in orbit in 1958. As director of the missile research facility in Alabama, von Braun supervised development of the Saturn V liquid-fuel rocket for Project Apollo. Von Braun was born in 1912 in Germany and joined a group of amateur rocket makers and launchers in Berlin in 1930. He was placed in charge of an experimental station in 1932 and received his Ph.D. degree in physics in 1934 from the University of Berlin. Von Braun developed a self-propelled, liquid-fuel flying bomb in 1938 which became known as the V-2 rocket. It was fired from German bases in France to the mainland of England and inflicted heavy damage to property and the civilian population.

After Germany surrendered in 1945, von Braun moved to the U.S. and was assigned as technical director of the U.S. Army missile proving grounds at White Sands, New Mexico. In 1950, he took charge of the missile research facility at Huntsville, Alabama, which became the U.S. Army Ordnance Guided Missile Division. Under von Braun's supervision, many rockets were developed, including the Redstone, Jupiter-C, and Jupiter. The first American satellite, *Explorer I*, was launched into orbit in 1958 by a modified Redstone missile. Von Braun wrote many articles on rockets. His books include *First Men to the Moon* (1960).

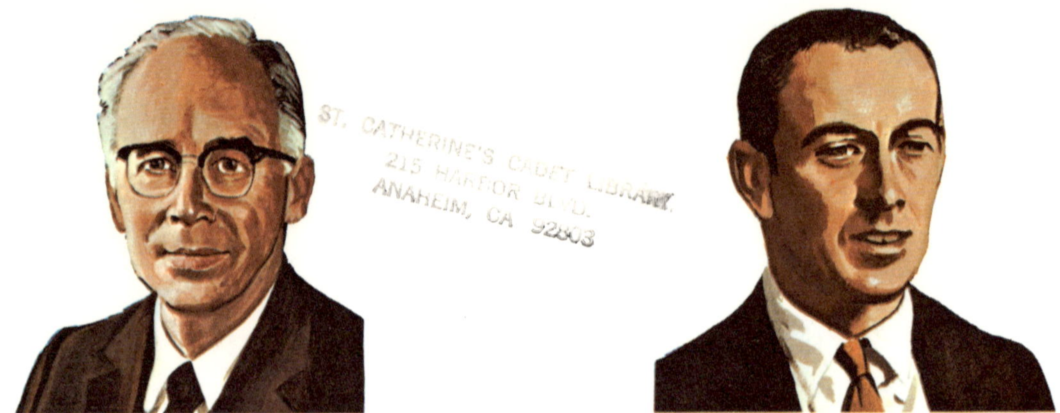

George Wald

James D. Watson

Wald, George. For his discovery of the chemical process by which retinal pigments in the human eye transmit light into sight, biochemist George Wald was awarded a share of the 1967 Nobel Prize in medicine. Studying the retina—the sensitive inside lining of the eye—and comparing it to film in a camera, Wald found that the two systems of reception cells in the retina are triggered into a response by light hitting the back of the eye. Studies of receptors (cones) and how they respond to bright light and transmit color, and how other receptors (rods) take over in dim light and transmit shades of gray led Wald in 1932 to discover that vitamin A exists in the retina. In the late 1940s he set out to duplicate the process of rod vision. Wald showed that a pigment in the rods, rhodopsin, consists of a protein in combination with a compound called retinene, and retinene is formed from vitamin A. He followed by revealing that when light strikes the rhodopsin pigment, the protein and retinene separate and recombine in the dark. Wald determined that vitamin A deficiency would impair performance of the rods and result in night blindness. He recommended that pilots eat foods rich in vitamin A, such as carrots.

Wald was born in New York in 1906 and received his Ph.D. from Columbia in 1932. After study in Europe, Wald joined the faculty of Harvard University in 1934. He began his study on the cones in the late 1950s and identified the pigments that are sensitive to red, yellow-green, and blue. Wald was elected to the National Academy of Sciences in 1950.

Watson, James D. By creating a model of deoxyribonucleic acid (DNA) in 1953, biochemist James Watson and a British associate helped solve the scientific mystery of how living cells reproduce themselves in their own likeness. For their discovery revealing the double helical (spiral) nature of the DNA molecule, Watson and geneticist Francis Crick were awarded the 1959 Nobel Prize in medicine. Watson was born in 1928, attended the University of Chicago, and received a Ph.D. from the University of Indiana in 1950. He was named a National Research Council fellow and studied in Europe, first at the University of Copenhagen and later at Cambridge University in England. Watson joined Crick at Cambridge in a series of genetic experiments, and they developed the idea of a DNA helical ladder, where one side of the helix determines the growth of the other side. Following an earlier study by Maurice Wilkins that indicated the spiral nature of the DNA molecule, they produced a DNA model in 1953 from colored beads, pieces of wire, and sheet metal. The model duplicated all the characteristics that would be needed for cell reproduction, and both scientists described their study in a short report.

Watson joined the Harvard University faculty in 1961 and published a technical study in his book *The Molecular Study of the Gene* (1965). He followed with a popular best-seller, *The Double Helix* (1968), which explains the significance of his discovery and the politics of science. Watson's later study was on the molecular structure of viruses.

George Hoyt Whipple **Robert B. Woodward** **Chen Ning Yang**

Whipple, George Hoyt. Studying the failure of some people to absorb vitamin B_{12}, which produces new red blood cells, medical researcher George Whipple started experiments in 1917 that later led to an effective treatment of the deadly disease of pernicious anemia. Born in 1878 in New Hampshire, Whipple graduated from Yale in 1900 and in 1905 earned his medical degree from Johns Hopkins University. He taught at Johns Hopkins until 1914, when he became professor of medicine at the University of California. Whipple organized the new medical school at the University of Rochester in New York in 1921. In his many years of anemia experiments, he bled dogs to induce the disease and then tried various foods to rebuild their blood. He found that liver produced one of the most effective remedies for anemia. Whipple shared the Nobel Prize in medicine with George R. Minot and W. P. Murphy in 1934.

Woodward, Robert B. By artificially creating a steroid in 1951, chemist Robert Woodward duplicated a natural fat-soluble organic compound and opened new studies of chemical processes in the human body. Experimenting at Harvard University, Woodward performed 20 chemical steps using 22 pounds of chemicals to produce a fraction of an ounce of his synthetic steroid. Woodward was born in 1917 in Boston and received his Ph.D. in 1937 from the Massachusetts Institute of Technology. He joined the Harvard faculty in 1940 and was awarded a full professorship in 1951. He made the first total synthesis of quinine in 1944, creating a new synthetic chemical which was an exact duplicate of natural quinine. Woodward synthesized chlorophyll, a substance found in all green plants, in 1960. For his research in organic chemistry, Woodward was awarded the Nobel Prize in chemistry in 1965.

Yang, Chen Ning. For his proof that a nuclear law, the conservation of parity, does not apply when small atomic particles are brought together, physicist Chen Ning Yang shared the Nobel Prize in physics in 1957. With his associate Tsung Dao Lee, Yang studied the theory of elementary particles and found that a particle's spin direction could be to the right or left, instead of following in one direction. Their studies made possible a more exact theory of elementary particles by showing that balance in an atomic reaction is not always required, as originally thought by other scientists. Yang was born in 1922 in China, came to the U.S. in 1945 on a scholarship, and received his Ph.D. at the University of Chicago in 1948. He was appointed to the Institute of Advanced Studies at Princeton in 1949 and in 1965 was elected to the Albert Einstein Chair in Science at the State University of New York at Stony Brook.

INDEX
TO SCIENTISTS BOOK